SUN TZU
for
WOMEN

孫
子

THE ART OF WAR
FOR WINNING
IN BUSINESS

BECKY SHEETZ-RUNKLE

BUSINESS

Avon, Massachusetts

Published by Adams Business,
an imprint of Adams Media, a division of F+W Media, Inc.
57 Littlefield Street, Avon, MA 02322. U.S.A.
www.adamsmedia.com

ISBN 10: 1-59869-907-5
ISBN 13: 978-1-59869-907-4
eISBN 10: 1-4405-1178-0
eISBN 13: 978-1-4405-1178-3

Printed in the United States of America.

10   9   8   7   6   5   4   3   2   1

Library of Congress Cataloging-in-Publication Data
Sheetz-Runkle, Becky.
Sun Tzu for women / Becky Sheetz-Runkle.
p. cm.
Includes bibliographical references.
ISBN-13: 978-1-59869-907-4   ISBN-10: 1-59869-907-5
ISBN-13: 978-1-4405-1178-3 (ebook)   ISBN-10: 1-4405-1178-0 (ebook)
1. Businesswomen. 2. Success in business. 3. Self-confidence. I. Title.
HD6053.S415   2011
650.1082—dc22   2010041350

This publication is designed to provide accurate and authoritative information with
regard to the subject matter covered. It is sold with the understanding that the publisher
is not engaged in rendering legal, accounting, or other professional advice. If legal
advice or other expert assistance is required, the services of a competent professional
person should be sought.

—From a *Declaration of Principles* jointly adopted by a Committee of the
American Bar Association and a Committee of Publishers and Associations

Many of the designations used by manufacturers and sellers to distinguish their
product are claimed as trademarks. Where those designations appear in this book and
Adams Media was aware of a trademark claim, the designations have been printed
with initial capital letters.

This book is available at quantity discounts for bulk purchases.
For information, please call 1-800-289-0963.

To Miriam—
My generous and loving mother.
She's survived cancer, difficult marriages, and a stubborn daughter.

And my teacher, *Soke* Randy Hutchins—
He's modeled how to be a martial artist, and a teacher, but most of all,
a wonderful and selfless human being.

Contents

Chapter 8: Innovation / 79

Chapter 9: Duty / 89

Chapter 10: Authenticity / 103

Chapter 11: Harness Deception to Shape Perception / 115

Chapter 12: Preparedness / 123

Chapter 13: Understand Yourself / 135

Chapter 14: Understanding and Leveraging Others / 149

Chapter 15: Practice the Basics / 161

Chapter 16: Battlefield Wisdom / 177

Chapter 17: Continuous Learning / 189

Chapter 1

Introduction to the Battlefield

孫子

About *The Art of War*

A masterpiece of military strategy, *The Art of War* was written by the Chinese philosopher-general Sun Tzu around 500 B.C. It contains thirteen short chapters totaling only 7,000 words, but its impact has been much larger than its size. Its teachings have shaped Eastern military and business thinking. In the West, the book's popularity continues to grow as managers and leaders seek to apply its principles to their business challenges.

About Sun Tzu

Very little is known about Sun Tzu. He was a great military strategist who committed a distinguished lifetime's worth of knowledge to bamboo strips. Or he never really existed at all. The book may have been written by a collection of men. In an embodiment of his battlefield strategy, Sun Tzu is a mystery.

Until clear evidence presents itself, believe the origin you wish. The battles were settled a long time ago. The man or men who wrote the book have long since turned to dust. The lessons are what remain.

About the Translation

The English translation of *The Art of War* used in *Sun Tzu for Women* is the same one used in *Sun Tzu: The Art of War for Managers: 50 Strategic*

Rules Updated for Today's Business, by Gerald A. Michaelson and Steven Michaelson (Adams Media). Alternate translations are included and noted when they offer useful interpretations of the material.

About *Sun Tzu for Women*

Sun Tzu for Women shows how sixteen core attributes from *The Art of War* can help women today achieve professional success.

This book doesn't extract ancient Eastern concepts and attempt to force-fit them into a modern Western context. Instead, real-life lessons from women who have survived and thrived in business illustrate Sun Tzu's timeless lessons.

Sun Tzu for Women captures the spirit of *The Art of War* and makes it eminently accessible, relevant, and applicable to women who live and work all over the world.

Why You Need *Sun Tzu for Women*

Men are taught to apologize for their weaknesses,
women for their strengths.
—LOIS WYSE

Around the world, executives and managers embrace *The Art of War*. Male executives and managers, that is. Sun Tzu's treatise on military strategy is rarely lauded as recommended reading for women. Maybe the harsh battlefield realities of a brilliant Chinese military strategist who lived five hundred years before Christ seem a long way from the cubicles, executive suites, and boardrooms of twenty-first-century female leaders. But following Sun Tzu's strategies can help women get the absolute best out of their careers and themselves.

Sun Tzu for Women isn't a black-and-white discussion of how military campaigns translate into customer acquisition or how Sun Tzu would create a Strengths, Weaknesses, Opportunities, and Threats (SWOT) analysis if he were in our boardrooms today. It's about how women can first *understand*, and then effectively *internalize*, Sun Tzu's strategies to advance their careers and improve their businesses. The pace of our lives, our worlds, and our workdays is often so frenetic that true understanding is elusive.

The Guide to Your Journey

If you believe victory is your only option, *Sun Tzu for Women* is for you. It will help you define and develop the mentality and inner tenacity that you need to reach the pinnacle of your potential, no matter where you are in your career now. *Sun Tzu for Women* is about the journey from who you are to who you can become.

It reconciles ancient truths with modern realities. It shares memorable battlefield, boardroom, and life experiences of powerful women from antiquity to modernity, and includes examples from the author's two decades of arduous martial arts training.

The scenarios Sun Tzu describes may be foreign to many readers. But the applications are familiar. Timeless truths, both simple and complex, never go out of style.

For Sun Tzu, victory begins well before the battle is fought. The woman who hasn't cultivated the spirit of self-belief will be unable to carry out any of the tactics. *Sun Tzu for Women* will change how you see yourself, your circumstances, and your business.

Your Competitive Advantage

Women need to study *The Art of War* because their male counterparts do. For years, businessmen have used its strategies to become more effective leaders and implementers. Women who make the mistake of seeing this battlefield classic as too military or too masculine will lose out on the benefits their colleagues are realizing.

Sharing Common Pitfalls

Collectively, women in business experience many of the same obstacles. Maybe you:

- Seek to avoid conflict
- Are unsure of which battles to fight and when to fight them
- Desire to stay in your comfort zone and keep the peace
- Experience confusion about being true to yourself or adopting traits characteristic of male leadership models
- Don't ask for what you want
- Allow timidity to prevent you from achieving big
- Fear the way boldness will be perceived by others
- Are prone to distraction from outside the office

Sun Tzu for Women explores what Sun Tzu himself says about such challenges. You'll learn how Carly Fiorina, Geraldine Laybourne, Meg Whitman, Drew Gilpin Faust, Condoleezza Rice, and many women like them overcame external obstacles to succeed.

Their stories, plus the latest research, will show you how to break through barriers—including those within yourself—to win battles, create opportunities, and expand your horizons.

Women Share Similar Success Attributes

In addition to facing similar obstacles, women also share similar attributes that lead to success, such as:

- Intuition
- Sensitivity
- Collaboration
- Passion
- Independence
- Team building

The challenge, however, is fully utilizing these strengths. *Sun Tzu for Women* will show you how.

Chapter 2

Indomitable Spirit

孫子

You must do the thing you think you cannot do.
—ELEANOR ROOSEVELT

> **THE BATTLE:** Insecurity will keep you from overcoming challenges. If you expect yourself to fall short, you'll be destined for failure. Character isn't about what happens to you, but how you respond to it.
>
> **THE CHAMPION:** If you're a winner, you have a spirit of victory in each battle. You know that with each challenge, you grow smarter, stronger, more resilient, and more capable of being who you're destined to be.

Indomitable spirit—the courage within that keeps you from defeat—is the soul of Sun Tzu's battlefield strategy. It must also be at the core of your business strategy. It makes or breaks armies and will do the same for you on a personal level. Victory is a state of mind forged in your experiences.

Indomitable isn't a word used very often in our culture. But it's a familiar concept if you strive for excellence. It's refusing to be conquered or overcome. You'll often have to find unconventional ways to defeat a larger, stronger, better-funded, or more-established enemy. No matter what, with an indomitable sprit, you resolve to win. There are no other options.

People who exhibit this kind of courage have had their spirits forged in adversity. Through their triumphs, they've developed the mindset that victory, ultimately, will always be theirs. But success has to be defined on your terms, not on anyone else's. Sometimes winning is simply about survival and going on to fight another day.

Sun Tzu says this about how to battle when the odds are against you: *If less in number, be capable of defending yourself. And if in all respects unfavorable, be capable of eluding him. Hence, a weak force will eventually fall captive to a strong one if it simply holds ground and conducts a desperate defense.*

There's a difference between being able to defend yourself, your team, or your organization, and desperately trying to survive. The first is a spirit of refusing to be overcome. The second is a spirit of chaos and confusion that leads to destruction.

Beginning by Winning

For Sun Tzu, victory is to be achieved before the battle is initiated. This is the embodiment of an unconquerable spirit: *A wise commander always ensures that his forces are put in an invincible position, and at the same time will be sure to miss no opportunity to defeat the enemy. It follows that a triumphant army will not fight with the enemy until the victory is assured, while an army destined to defeat will always fight with the opponent first, in the hope that it may win by sheer good luck.*

This scenario illustrates the concept of beginning by winning:

Two athletes have trained hard for a difficult race. They're both in excellent shape. Both women suffered various injuries during their years of running—shin splits, knee problems, and pulled hamstrings. They each have personal lives and jobs that demand their attention and cause them daily stress.

Generally speaking, the same things have *happened to them*. The difference is in how each responds. Throughout the first woman's training, she's been ready to win. She arrives on race day with single-purpose focus. She's not thinking about the injuries that have plagued her. She has one thing on her mind—winning.

The second woman has worked just as hard. Long hours. Late nights at the gym. Early mornings on the road. She's thinking about winning too. But that's not all she's thinking about. She's thinking about what will happen if she doesn't win. After all, if she falls short, it will probably be because of her injuries. Or because it's hard to focus after that awful fight she had with her husband last night. And then there's the stress of her son's performance in school. Will he be able to get into a good college? Yes, she's in great shape and is well-prepared. But she believes that if she doesn't win, there's a good reason why. She has given herself permission to fail. It won't be her fault if she's not up to par. It'll be her hamstring, or her husband, or her son.

Who do you think will have the better race?

Big-Time Risks, Big-Time Rewards

High achievers take serious risks and overcome major obstacles to realize awesome returns. While Sun Tzu calls for always being in a stronger position, he acknowledges that there will be battles where the odds against you are great. Champions of the business battlefield understand this kind of adversity. They know what it's like to go up against a difficult, seemingly insurmountable opponent. And they know what it means to defeat that opponent, and, in so doing, conquer themselves.

While women are often deemed more cautious than their male counterparts, data doesn't support the idea that women are risk averse.

Women take on more personal debt to fund businesses than do men. For three decades, women have been starting companies at twice the rate of men. The growth, employment, and revenue rates of these businesses have outpaced the economy.

Former Hewlett-Packard CEO Carly Fiorina famously transformed the culture of her company from risk aversion to risk taking. She led HP to return to its roots of innovation. Critics attacked her when she took a major risk in leading HP's controversial merger with Compaq Computer Corp. But today this is regarded as a powerhouse merger success story. By her terms, her legacy is one of success. From HP, she's branched out into politics, one of the most dangerous minefields in America for a woman.

Taking risks requires calculating danger. Sun Tzu urges an accurate and comprehensive picture of battlefield conditions, including the resilience of the enemy. To be victorious, he says, you must study the spirit of your opponent: *A whole army may be robbed of its spirit, and its commander deprived of his presence of mind. Now, at the beginning of a campaign, the spirit of soldiers is keen; after a certain period of time, it declines; and in the later stage, it may be dwindled to naught. A clever commander, therefore, avoids the enemy when his sprit is keen and attacks him when it is lost.*

In addition to your resolute purpose and commitment to success, be mindful of the courage, resilience, and commitment of your adversaries. Time your risks appropriately.

Passion Fuels the Spirit

Every woman has her own sources of motivation and inspiration. What are yours? If your goal is to be exceptional, to develop and leverage your indomitable spirit, then passion must be at the core of what you do and why you do it. You must care deeply about who you work for and with.

If you're in an industry you love, but working for or with people you don't believe in, you won't sustain your passion for long.

According to the National Foundation for Women Business Owners, most women who transition out of corporate careers into their own endeavors do so for one reason: independence.

These women have chosen to move on from positions where they feel undervalued, underestimated, and unsatisfied. They trade up to more demanding jobs and better realize their potential. Margaret Heffernan is a five-time CEO who has interviewed hundreds of entrepreneurs for her book, *How She Does It*. She puts it this way: "It is an existential flight to a place where who and what they are, how they like to work, and the things they care about are not just tolerated but are given a dynamic and central role."

For women like these, passion is critical. If you're good, you deserve to be in a position where the things you care about matter.

Your passion defines who you are. It will give you the stamina to win victory after victory. Your work reveals what you care about and the depth of your commitment. What does your passion and how you apply it to your work say about you?

Ten Times Down, Eleven Times Up

Sun Tzu emphasizes the importance of seizing opportunities, no matter what the circumstances. As Lionel Giles translates: *If, on the other hand, in the midst of difficulties we are always ready to seize an advantage, we may extricate ourselves from misfortune.*

Even when the challenges you face seem too daunting, look for ways to win. The strong leader knows that with each victory and each defeat she lives through and learns from, she grows more capable of reaching her full potential. "Ten times down, eleven times up," is the philosophy of those who've triumphed over obstacles.

Despite how well it prepares us for what lies ahead, we rarely view adversity as a good thing. Naturally, we want to avoid difficulty, but conflict and trials should be viewed as opportunities. They're chances to learn, grow, and excel. Without conflict and adversity, you'll never know what you're capable of.

Elizabeth I, the sixteenth-century queen of England, could relate to this. In her culture, fear and suspicion were commonplace. Her mother, Anne Boleyn, was unjustly executed for treason when her father, Henry VIII, wished to marry Jane Seymour. When Elizabeth was sixteen, she was accused of plotting against her half-brother, Edward VI. She sustained days of relentless interrogation but wouldn't confess.

The painful experiences of her childhood and young adulthood shaped her into the powerful monarch she'd become. As queen, she would always project strength and indomitable sprit.

Learn to Fall

Falling hurts. In the martial arts, many people quit when they realize how difficult it is to learn to fall. This is a hurdle they won't let themselves overcome. But for those who stick with their training, these painful lessons become much easier. Over time, as the student learns to fall correctly, even the hardest throws and takedowns become easy to take.

When you know how to fall properly, you no longer experience the rough spots. You no longer get the wind knocked out of you. You no longer get headaches, bruised elbows, and banged tailbones from the impact. Or, at least, you experience these pains *less* frequently. You still feel them when you're unprepared or thrown with unexpected force.

It's from falling down that you learn to win, including how not to get taken off your feet in the same way again. You become better, and your footing is more sure. You learn who to trust and who not to trust by who knocks you down and who helps (or doesn't help) you up. You learn the strength of your spirit.

Get Back Up—Quickly

In the executive suite, as in every facet of your life, you're not defeated in falling down, but in failing to get back up. The only way to get back on your feet is in your attitude, perseverance, and unwillingness to allow even a crushing blow to seal your fate. Getting back up is at the core of solid character. It sends a message to both friends and enemies that as long as you have breath in your lungs, you will *always* get back up.

Sun Tzu understands that defeat may happen. But the great can find victory in losing by getting back up, regrouping, innovating, and moving on stronger than ever before. That's the spirit of victory.

Timing is critical for Sun Tzu. When you get knocked down, get up quickly. Don't make it easy for your enemies. Instead of dwelling on failure and spending too much time in nonproductive, defeated positions, get up and move forward. Women who allow others' negative comments to linger, causing pain and resentment, also compromise their ability to overcome defeat. As Sun Tzu says, ***Do not linger on critical ground.***

Adapt to Getting Choked

If you're a martial artist, the first time you feel yourself in a good, tight choke, you panic. You feel like you're going to die. You can't breathe. Your heart races. You feel helpless. You may be in a great deal of pain. But even severe and vivid pain is muted by what's going on inside your mind. Your body is screaming, amidst a variety of expletives, "YOU ARE GOING TO DIE!"

You lose firm footing and can't fight back. If the opponent takes you off your feet, you'll lose your balance. Once your peripheral vision starts to blacken, it's only a matter of short seconds before you lose consciousness. If the person choking you doesn't let up, everything fades to black.

Even in the controlled, relatively safe environment of a *dojo* (training studio), getting choked for the first time is a harrowing experience. The next few times, it's still very scary, but you find yourself adapting and panicking less and less with each subsequent choke. You eventually learn how to counter chokes and escape. You're no longer defenseless. Instead of your mind insisting that you're going to die, you process, "Okay, you've been here before. Let's get out of this." You're still in a terribly disadvantageous position, but it's familiar and you have a plan for escape.

Whether you're a young entrepreneur or leading a *Fortune* 500 company, the first time you're faced with an experience in which things take a very bad turn, panic may set in. You may feel defenseless. When you lose a big client, a promising deal falls through, or a threatening acquisition is announced, you feel that suffocating, constricting sensation. You momentarily lose your ability to think clearly. Mentally, and maybe even physically, you may flail about, at a loss for how to respond.

But, as Sun Tzu directs, *do not linger on critical ground*. Learn from your trials, so the next time a potentially devastating blow comes, you can maneuver to take the pressure off. You can breathe during the brief moments you created, and quickly reason through the situation. You've been here before.

When Patience Isn't a Virtue

Most women are raised to comply with standards of passivity and patience. You were probably conditioned to wait to be asked to dance and to be asked to get married. You probably heard, "Mind your manners. Be polite. Be patient." Social grace is a great virtue in business, and in the rest of your life. But there's a time to be patient and polite, and there's a time to put your unbreakable spirit into overdrive, act decisively, and move ahead without yielding.

Conditions for moving to the next level may never be ideal. But Sun Tzu calls you to be perceptive and move with intensity when the time is right: *An army superior in strength takes action like the bursting of pent-up waters into a chasm of a thousand fathoms deep. This is what the disposition of military strength means in the actions of war.*

BATTLEFIELD CHALLENGE

1. Think about your last and greatest period of adversity. What did you learn about yourself in your response? How can you apply what you learned to your next great trial?

2. Can you relate to the second runner? Do you ever give yourself permission to fail? How different do you think the results would be if you approached battles like the first runner?

3. Are you passionate about your work? If not, what changes do you have to make to bring out your best?

The Unbreakable Human Spirit of Harriet Tubman

Strength isn't measured purely in numbers. It's also measured in human spirit. Harriet Tubman acted with all the dynamism and unstoppable force of pent-up waters and saw victory based on the strength of her sprit. She didn't wait for permission, perfect opportunities to be presented, or promises of safety. Instead, she put her passion into action. "General" Tubman, the first woman in American history to plan and lead a military campaign, freed thousands of slaves during her life.

A runaway slave best known as a conductor on the Underground Railroad during the Civil War, Tubman made nineteen trips into the South to usher more than 300 slaves to freedom over ten years. The threats she faced were terrifying and the circumstances overwhelming. But her spirit was greater.

Tubman's life was defined by service to others. As a slave in her early teens, she blocked a doorway to protect a field hand from an angry overseer. When the overseer threw a weight at the field hand, it hit the protective Tubman instead. She carried this head injury with her throughout her life.

Tubman developed innovative techniques to rescue slaves. She took the master's buggy for the first part of the journey and left on a Saturday night, since newspapers didn't advertise runaway notices until Monday. When confronted by slave hunters, she turned and headed back south, where they'd least expect a slave rescuer to go. She was, after all, very much a wanted woman. Her capture would have brought a $40,000 reward. She carried a drug to use on crying babies and a gun to use on slaves who threatened to give up. "You'll be free or die," she told them. Tubman used code to communicate with the people she freed, including singing songs that alerted them for when to stay hidden and when to travel.

In addition to being a cook, nurse, and spy for the Union Army, Tubman was a warrior. In 1863, she led a successful military raid of black soldiers along the Combahee River. The campaign liberated 750 slaves and destroyed several prominent slave owners' plantations.

Tubman allowed her adversaries to underestimate her. She pretended to be mentally slow so no one would buy her. She got the nickname Moses on the Underground Railroad. Since slave owners thought Moses must be a man, she didn't bother trying to correct the misconception. To protect her identity, she sometimes dressed as a man, or as an old woman hobbling along. This deception helped her spy most effectively on the Confederate Army.

Her indomitable spirit is summed up in her quest for liberty for herself and her people: "There were two things I had a right to, liberty and death. If I could not have one, I would have the other, for no man should take me alive."

She embodied Sun Tzu's words: *Throw them in a perilous situation and they will survive; put them in desperate ground and they will live. For when the army is placed in such a situation, it can snatch victory from defeat.*

Chapter 3

The Quest for Excellence

孫子

The secret of joy in work is contained in
one word—excellence. To know how to do something
well is to enjoy it.
—PEARL BUCK

> **THE BATTLE:** Complacency is the enemy of excellence. If your
> expectations are low, you'll never be excellent, or even good.
> Excellence means using your brilliance, passion, and talent,
> and setting and internalizing sky-high goals. Importantly, this
> means putting yourself in a position to achieve greatness. The
> idea of positioning yourself to win is echoed throughout *The
> Art of War.*
>
> **THE CHAMPION:** If your standard is excellence, you think big
> and execute well. You'll always be in high demand.

The *Art of War* is a challenge to achieve the ideal state of flawless
execution based on a range of highly developed attributes: *When
campaigning, be swift as the wind; in leisurely march, be majestic as
the forest; in raiding and plundering, be fierce as fire; in standing, be*

firm as the mountains. When hiding, be as unfathomable as things behind the clouds; when moving, fall like a thunderclap.

Sun Tzu provides a model of perfection for the superior leader. While the standards you set for yourself should be very high, they should be obtainable. Sun Tzu's wisdom, combined with the realities of your twenty-first-century struggles, can help you realize that balance.

Be Twice as Good

Excellence is about much more than working harder than the next person. "Better than so-and-so" is on par with "good enough." Excellence doesn't mean working around the clock in hopes that your boss will notice your commitment and loyalty, either. It means setting the standard for everyone else to follow. To do this, you have strive to be twice as good.

How is this accomplished? Acclaimed real estate mogul Barbara Corcoran put it like this: "Forget the fact that you're a woman and out-hustle everyone else. Being an entrepreneur is all about hustling harder and persevering longer than the next guy. Whether you're a girl or a guy makes no difference."

Your standard should be excellence because that's what you expect from yourself. It should also be greatness because, as Nina DiSesa, chairman and chief creative officer of McCann New York, said, that's what it's going to take: "As long as men and women are different, as long as we are battling one another for the top jobs, there will always be a double standard. Everything men and women do will be judged differently…We must always work smarter, think better, manage more humanely, and be more patient than our male counterparts. This is the price we pay for joining their club."

Despite these two accomplished professionals' differing perspectives, the bottom line is that if you want to be victorious, you have to be twice as good. And to be truly excellent, you must be in an environment that values achievement. Sun Tzu writes repeatedly on the importance of being in a location where you can succeed. You may have grand dreams, but if you're not in a position to reach them, they'll only ever be dreams. You must seize and maintain the dominant position. Keep focused on what you want and arrive there before your competitors, be they rival companies or rivals on your way to the top: *One who occupies the field of battle first and awaits the enemy is at ease.*

Identify Weaknesses—and Move On!

To achieve your full potential, you must identify and analyze your weak points: *If in the neighborhood of your camp there are dangerous defiles or ponds and low-lying ground overgrown with aquatic grass and reeds, or forested mountains with dense tangled undergrowth, they must be thoroughly searched, for these are possible places where ambushes are laid and spies are hidden.*

It's the natural inclination for most of us to spend more time on what we're good at, and less time in the tangled undergrowth and swamps, but that's not a strategy for excellence. Not only will this shortsightedness keep you from climbing the corporate ladder, but it will leave your weaknesses vulnerable to exploitation by others.

The Perfection Paradox

Talking about excellence is easy. Achieving it is tough. But if excellence is difficult, perfection is elusive at best. After a lot of practice and focus, you may grasp perfection for a moment, only to have it slip through your fingers, like vapor. Sword instructor Sensei David Drawdy put it in a way I'll never forget. "You'll never really achieve perfection. You may perform a technique perfectly for a moment. Enjoy that moment—because it will be gone forever," he said. Perfection can't be grasped or held. It quickly goes from *is* to *was*. This is an important lesson for many women who hold themselves to unobtainable standards, never allowing themselves to appreciate or enjoy their many achievements. These women internalize problems and dwell on failures.

Don't Dwell

Marion Luna Brem, owner of a multimillion-dollar auto dealership empire, has noticed that when women don't make the sale, their tendency is to say, "What's wrong with me?"

But, she says, a man more often asks, "What's wrong with *them*?" This is a fascinating disparity. (While Brem notes that men and women deal with rejection differently, men don't necessarily cope with it *better*.)

Learning from mistakes is a virtue. But spending so much time on what you think you did wrong, something hurtful someone else said, or a difficult client's latest tirade, isn't at all beneficial. It's damaging. Dwelling on your mistakes depletes your strength and your spirit, two things you need daily for doing battle.

Get Real

Robin Wolaner, the founder of *Parenting* magazine, has seen women sabotage themselves into thinking of all the ways they're not perfect for a job opportunity. Men, by contrast, are less inclined to have this qualification crisis. Her advice is to not compare yourself to the ideal candidate. Compare yourself to the other *real* ones. They aren't perfect either. This applies to much more than job interviews.

Banish Victim Mindsets

You may think that being a soldier means carrying out orders no matter what. But Sun Tzu says this isn't so: *If the sovereign heeds these stratagems of mine and acts upon them, he will surely win the war, and I shall, therefore, stay with him. If the sovereign neither heeds nor acts upon them, he will certainly suffer defeat, and I shall leave.*

A soldier has self-determination. So do you. However, many women have mental perspectives that make it difficult to see that they're in charge of their lives and their fates. As *Dancing on the Glass Ceiling* authors Candy Deemer and Nancy Fredericks point out, these "mental barriers" are:

- Seeing everything as happening *to* you
- Being overly critical of yourself and focusing on your failings
- Minimizing your achievements
- Embracing the status quo and being unwilling to challenge it

If you find yourself succumbing to any of these barriers, you'll never achieve your best. If you struggle with one or more of these, you must begin by identifying this as a weakness. This is a critical aspect of Chapter 13: "Understand Yourself."

Zanshin—Finish as Well as You Start

Anybody can sketch out a rough business plan on a bar napkin. It doesn't take great skill to come up with a concept and get excited by our unsubstantiated great ideas. But even the best concepts can fall apart at execution. Sun Tzu recognizes the inability to follow through as worse than a miscalculation: *Now, to win battles and capture lands and cities but to fail to consolidate these achievements is ominous and may be described as a waste of resources and time.*

The Japanese concept of *zanshin* is translated as "remaining spirit" or "continued concentration." It's better experienced than explained. But let's give it a shot.

For a martial artist, after you complete a technique, whether it's a throw or a cut with a sword, you remain in a fully aware state. You're both completely fixed on the technique you've just performed, and completely aware of the next attack that may come. You're not anticipating either, but open to any possibility.

Another important component of zanshin is following through. If a technique starts out well, but ends poorly, then zanshin cannot be achieved. The end is as important as the beginning.

Maintain Enthusiasm

Many business relationships begin with high expectations and promises of delivery. The service provider is enthusiastic at the beginning, but loses excitement as work drives on and the project continues. Relationships sometimes become fractured. These developments aren't good for short-term delivery or the longer-term relationship.

To be excellent, you must keep the concept of "continued concentration" in mind to deliver on your commitments and create valuable relationships. Maintain your enthusiasm for a major new customer, exciting new project, or energizing promotion, even after the proverbial honeymoon is over. On your good days and bad days, make it your standard to finish as well as you start.

To Finish Well, Begin with Goals

Finishing well begins with clearly defined goals. Sharon Hadary, former executive director of the Center for Women's Business Research, points to research indicating that for entrepreneurs, setting growth goals is "the only statistically significant predictor of business growth." It's not the industry, the size of the business, or the number of years in business. It's the growth goal.

Hadary points out that the training many entrepreneurs receive at women's business centers, conferences and seminars for female entrepreneurs, and adult-education courses often ignores growth planning.

Instead, it focuses on the common advice start-ups receive, such as marketing and personal budget planning. Excellence begins with ambitious goals.

The Dangers of Complacency

It's always disappointing to see people who've allowed complacency to atrophy their skills. These people appear interested only in going through the motions and doing as little as possible. They'll prepare the report or manage the account, but don't expect anything more than the status quo. Even the best can fall into this trap.

A memorable picture of these consequences was at a demonstration where two jujitsu masters exhibited their skills. Both had solid reputations for great proficiency. Each of these men had trained for decades and was a very serious practitioner.

But it turned out that, despite similar backgrounds and years in training, there was a great difference between the two of them. One had precise timing and accuracy. In lockstep with Sun Tzu's standard, his movements were flawless. If he did make mistakes, he moved so elegantly and effortlessly that no one would have known it. It was a thrill to watch him.

The second instructor paled by comparison. He was far less precise, his timing was off, and he moved with greater effort. He was sluggish and lethargic. His mistakes were evident. Throughout the demonstration, it appeared that he fought himself much more than he did any opponent.

What had happened to the second master? He had not been actively training. He had suffered some injuries and allowed himself to get lazy. It showed.

The reality is that no matter how good you were yesterday, no matter how much you accomplished, you must be prepared to do battle today. Let yourself slip, fail to keep up, ignore your weaknesses, compromise your integrity, and people will notice. Your enemies will follow Sun

Tzu's advice and overtake you at your weakest: *A clever commander, therefore, avoids the enemy when his spirit is keen and attacks him when it is lost.*

Sun Tzu's standard is unflinching excellence. Because battles are won and lost on "small" mistakes, miscalculations, and poor preparation, he requires exceptional action at every turn. The emphasis you place on staying sharp and always being ready to do battle will make all the difference.

Inexhaustible Excellence

While peak performance is the goal, there are limits to human stamina. Just as athletes rest after competitions, you need time to regroup and recharge. Long hours are fatiguing. Continuous presentations that require you to be your sharpest wear you down. Grueling meetings zap your enthusiasm. Living through mergers, acquisitions, downsizing, and rapid growth demand all you have to give. How can you be excellent when you're at the end of the line?

Excellence doesn't mean being sharp every waking moment. It means being at your best when it matters most. It also requires knowing when your opponents are at their weakest and capitalizing on those opportunities. As Sun Tzu says, a smart general attacks the enemy when his spirit is at its weakest. Spirit and stamina fade. If you work yourself to the brink of physical and emotional limits as a matter of course, you're setting yourself up for failure and making yourself vulnerable to attack. If every day is a marathon, you won't be extraordinary in your every action. You must know when to go all out and when to reserve your energy.

Sun Tzu is talking about leveraging an army here, but its applications for your life are many: *Generally, in battle, use the normal force to engage and use the extraordinary to win. Now, to a commander adept at the use of extraordinary forces, his resources are as infinite as heaven and earth, as inexhaustible as the flow of the running rivers.*

Use your extraordinary ability in matters that call for them, and your normal energy when the extraordinary isn't a benefit. Sun Tzu reiterates this idea: *In battle, there are not more than two kinds of postures—operation of the extraordinary force and operation of the normal force, but their combinations give rise to an endless series of maneuvers. For these two forces are mutually reproductive. It is like moving in a circle, never coming to an end. Who can exhaust the possibilities of their combinations?*

Use your extraordinary energy, creativity, stamina, and skills to win. Use your normal energy in your day-to-day engagements. This way you'll be strong and sharp when it's required, and maximize your finite bandwidth.

BATTLEFIELD CHALLENGE

1. Are you well positioned to win battles and advance your territory? Are you at an organization that values excellence?
2. Do you identify with any of the mental barriers that may keep you from self-determination? If so, what will you do to overcome them?
3. How can you apply zanshin to your career, latest project, or team? List three times when you've not finished as well as you started. What was the consequence?

Carly Fiorina:
A Career Defined by Excellence

When Carly Fiorina dropped out of law school, her mother feared her daughter would never amount to anything. These are the kinds of things mothers say when they're disappointed or scared for their children. Fiorina's father wasn't pleased either. To him, quitting was failure. Here she was, 22 years old, a history (medieval, at that, one of your less marketable histories) and philosophy major. Fiorina had no experience in business and no exposure to it growing up. Still, it wouldn't be long before she would become the first woman to run a *Fortune* 20 company.

Her first post–law school job was as a receptionist in a commercial property brokerage firm. She learned there to focus on doing the best with the job she had, instead of thinking about the next job. She explored the possibilities there and went on to train to become a broker, then to get her MBA.

It's clear from Fiorina's career that excellence has been her standard. She went on to lead Lucent to an initial public offering, and become president of its largest business. But she's best known for her legacy at Hewlett-Packard. She was chairman and CEO of HP during the pivotal dot-com years from 1999 to 2005. She reinvented the company, doubling HP's revenues to $88 billion, with improved profitability across the board. Today, HP is the largest tech company in the world. For Fiorina, excellence is reached by refusing to acquiesce to boundaries. She wrote in a *New York Times* article, "Understand that the only limits that really matter are those you put on yourself, or that a business puts on itself. Most people and businesses are capable of far more than they realize."

Despite her very public firing from HP, Fiorina looks back with pride in her accomplishments at HP in a culture averse to change. "The worst thing I could have imagined happened. I lost my job in the most public way possible, and the press had a field day with it all over the world. And guess what? I'm still here. I am at peace and my soul is intact," she reflected shortly after the famous transition.

With her soul intact and plenty of experience with the media and critics, she's applying her vision, focus, and standard of excellence to the next phase of her life, politics.

Chapter 4

Technique— Your Advantage

孫子

Dr. Mark Sloan: "Aren't you gonna get in there?
If you wanna be chief, you gotta fight with the big boys."

Dr. Addison Montgomery Shepherd:
"Oh, I intend to fight like a girl. I'll let them kill each other
and then I'll be the only one left standing."
— *GREY'S ANATOMY*, ABC TELEVISION

THE BATTLE: To achieve victory, you may have to compete against much larger and better-funded opponents. You may have to battle entrenched cultural beliefs that require you to be twice as good. Don't play by the same rules as everybody else or try to force yourself to fit to artificial standards.

THE CHAMPION: Use your attributes and assets. Challenge— even change the rules if you must—and you'll succeed.

How you fight your battles is critical in determining the final outcome. There's elegance within all good strategy. To win, you need grace and technique.

Science According to Sun Tzu

The textbook definition of force is "velocity times mass equals force." All things being equal, the bigger, quicker mover will inflict more damage than the smaller and/or slower mover.

But for Sun Tzu, and for you, there's more to the story. Study and apply these lessons and they'll have a profound impact on how you fight your boardroom battles.

Timing

Sun Tzu teaches that opportunities must be seized when you're ready and when your opponent is not: *Invincibility lies in the defense; the possibility of victory in the attack. Defend yourself when the enemy's strength is abundant, and attack the enemy when it is inadequate.*

Timing means alertness to opportunities that are presented to you, as well as readiness to create them: *Thus, one who is adept at keeping the enemy on the move maintains deceitful appearances, according to which the enemy will act. He lures with something that the enemy is certain to take. By so doing he keeps the enemy on the move and then waits for the right moment to make a sudden ambush with picked troops.*

Sun Tzu's advice on using "picked troops" to make the ambush is important. Trust the right people with essential tasks when timing and action are critical.

Seize Opportunities

Acting decisively and definitively greatly boosts your odds of meeting an unprepared adversary. Sun Tzu tells us to take advantage of every viable and authentic opportunity: *If the enemy leaves a door open, you must rush in. Seize the place the enemy values without making an appointment to battle with him. Be flexible and decide your line of action according to the situation on the enemy side.*

Your readiness to capitalize on opponents' mistakes and your advantageous conditions, even amidst unfavorable circumstances, can make all the difference. Sun Tzu says: *If, on the other hand, in the midst of difficulties we are always ready to seize an advantage, we may extricate ourselves from misfortune.*

Prepare for Consequences

Of course, not everyone takes advantage of opportunities. Fear of consequences can be a major barrier. You may ask yourself, "What if the timing isn't right? What if I'll get hurt in the process? What if I fail?"

These are questions that are to be answered as you prepare yourself for battle. Once you've done your research and the opportunity is worth seizing, the time for asking questions is over. Rush in through the open door.

Robin Wolaner notes that among the many women she interviewed for *Naked in the Boardroom*, success wasn't about their personal career plan. Rather, in a word, she said, it was about "serendipity." Take advantage of every viable opportunity every time.

Create Opportunities

Capitalizing on opponents' missteps is important. So is shaping their perceptions to help create those openings: *At first, then, exhibit the coyness of a maiden until the enemy gives you an opening; afterwards be swift as a running hare, and it will be too late for the enemy to oppose you.*

Speed

Speed is part of the original equation for achieving force, and Sun Tzu emphasizes the importance of moving quickly to overtake an unprepared adversary: *Speed is the essence of war. Take advantage of the enemy's unpreparedness, make your way by unexpected routes, and attack him where he has taken no precautions.*

But moving quickly doesn't mean acting rashly, particularly when it comes to difficult territories—as in this case, walled cities: *The general unable to control his impatience will order his troops to swarm up the wall like ants with the result that one third of them are slain, while the cities remain untaken.*

Unleash Energy

This is the culmination of timing, seizing opportunities, creating opportunities, and speed. In times of battle, attacks should be let loose with ferocity, according to Sun Tzu: *An army of superior strength takes action like the bursting of pent-up waters into a chasm of a thousand fathoms deep. This is what the disposition of military strength means in actions of war.*

Wisely unleashing energy involves using the momentum of your people to exploit battlefield conditions. This can include your opponent's unpreparedness, changing market conditions, opportunities created by shifts in leadership, or crisis and controversy experienced by your competitor. Sun Tzu says: *He who takes advantage of the situation uses his men in fighting as rolling logs or rocks. It is the nature of logs and rocks to stay stationary on the flat ground, and to roll forward on a slope. If four-cornered, they stop; if round-shaped, they roll. Thus, the energy of troops skillfully commanded is just like the momentum of round rocks quickly tumbling down from a mountain thousands of feet in height. This is what "use of energy" means.*

Be prepared to exploit opportunities and put momentum, timing, and action on your side: *When torrential water tosses boulders, it is because of its momentum; when the strike of a hawk breaks the body of its prey, it is because of timing. Thus, in battle, a good commander creates a posture releasing an irresistible and overwhelming momentum, and his attack is precisely timed in a quick tempo. The energy is similar to a fully drawn crossbow; the timing, the release of the trigger.*

Spirit

There's more to directed force than physical factors. An essential element of force is spirit: *Throw your soldiers into a position whence there is no escape, and they will choose death over desertion. For if prepared to die, how can the officers and men not exert their uttermost strength to fight? In a desperate situation, they fear nothing; when there is no way out, they stand firm. Deep in a hostile land they are bound together. If there is no help for it, they will fight hard.*

Beyond just the physical, you must create and seize mental and spiritual conditions necessary to attain victory.

Size Doesn't (Always) Matter

Size is far from the only or most important factor for Sun Tzu: *In war, numbers alone confer no advantage. If one does not advance by force recklessly, and is able to concentrate his military power through a correct assessment of the enemy situation and enjoys full support of his men, that would suffice.*

Legendary mixed martial arts champion Royce Gracie provides an example of how technique, preparation, and concentrated skill can defy expectations and overcome larger challenges.

In the first Ultimate Fighting Championship (UFC), and others that followed, viewers and opponents were stunned when this comparatively little guy defeated competitor after competitor who consistently outweighed him by more than fifty pounds. In full-contact fighting, all things being equal, the big guy wins. All things being less equal, the bigger guy still usually wins.

Gracie won three UFC titles and is the only mixed martial artist to ever defeat four opponents in one night.

In Gracie's success, we see some of Sun Tzu's principles in action. Like this champion, you can compensate for lack of size, funding, and reputation by attacking definitively and quickly, harnessing your opponents' momentum, and multiplying it with your own. You can use techniques your opponents are unfamiliar with and unprepared to defend against. You can make up for what you lack in size and strength with technique and skill. In this way, you will embody Sun Tzu's "use of energy."

Know Your Strengths

Women share many traits and strengths that can be used to their advantage in business. These traits include collaboration, relationship building, communication, emotional intelligence, and creativity, among others. Recognizing and making the most of these assets will help you in big ways.

Collaboration and Relationship Building

Covered in detail in Chapter 14: "Understanding and Leveraging Others," collaboration, consensus, and team building are fundamental feminine traits. Former eBay CEO Meg Whitman is a well-known example of using a collaborative and nurturing leadership style. Tom Tierney, an eBay board member, said Whitman saw her job "as a leader to help other people succeed rather than to help herself succeed." In calling her a "chief executive enabler," Tierney highlights the impact of her methods on eBay's culture.

Building good teams and enabling the people under you to succeed is virtuous for Sun Tzu too: *He whose generals are able and not interfered with by the sovereign will win.*

Communication

An aptitude for communication is an outgrowth of collaboration. Women typically have an advantage in picking up on verbal and nonverbal cues. What people say and don't say is critical in every business transaction.

Sun Tzu calls for clear communication for armies to function smoothly and avoid threats: *If the army is confused and suspicious, neighboring rulers will take advantage of this and cause trouble. This is simply bringing anarchy into the army and flinging victory away.*

Emotional Intelligence

The consulting firm TalentSmart conducted a study of men and women that examined the emotional quotient (EQ) of each. EQ is a measurement of emotional intelligence, which is your capacity—and by some measurements, your perceived capacity—to identify, assess, manage, and control your emotions, others' emotions, and the emotions of groups.

The research shows that women score higher than men in overall emotional intelligence in three out of four skills measured: self-management, social awareness, and relationship management. In the fourth category, self-awareness, men and women score evenly. The social awareness and relationship management categories are indicators of skill in reading others and sensitivity in detecting when a problem exists.

Intuition

The intrinsic intuition many women possess is a decision-making advantage. The question for many women isn't whether or not they have intuition, but how well they trust and use it. According to the Center for Women's Business Research, "The highest-ranked factor influencing women entrepreneurs when making business decisions is being sure they have all the relevant information and data available." Second is whether or not the decision is consistent with a strong gut feeling. In an illustration of the collaborative leadership style of many women, the third factor is confidence that the outcome will be desirable and agree with the advice of trusted colleagues and external advisers.

Hope and feelings are by no means synonymous with intuition. Again, Sun Tzu tells us the difference is as stark as triumph and defeat:

It follows that a triumphant army will not fight with the enemy until the victory is assured, while an army destined to defeat will always fight with the opponent first, in the hope that it may win by sheer good luck.

The cofounder and former chairman and CEO of Oxygen Media, Geraldine Laybourne, saw how intuition and a gut instinct played out during her career. When she was president of Disney/ABC Cable Networks, the company had what she calls "an army of strategic planners who had no real operational experience."

Their modus operandi was to run the business purely by analysis and numbers. But, she said, "Your gut is often better without a lot of analysis than it is with. You can prove anything through analysis."

For Marsha Serlin, founder of United Scrap Metal, her gut has always been valuable in decision-making. "Women are very intuitive, and women do such a great job of knowing when to get in or get out of something," she believes. "Don't listen to anyone but your heart. If you think you can do it, you can do it. Most people will tell you that you can't, and that's probably the most debilitating part. Don't investigate your idea until it's dead—jump in with both feet. You'll never be sorry if you follow your dream."

Creativity

Everybody's creative, including people who don't think they are. Those people just haven't learned how to apply their personal creativity to get results. Creative thinking can bring you victory with minimum effort. Here's an example of how the well-known sixteenth-century Japanese samurai, Tsukahara Bokuden, used his creativity to beat an adversary:

One beautiful day, Bokuden was aboard a ferry crossing a lake. Another passenger, also a samurai, was looking for a fight. He asked Bokuden what style of swordsmanship he studied. Bokuden replied, *Mutekatsu Ryu*, or, "the style of winning without a sword."

The bully found this to be ridiculous, and as bullies do, continued to badger Bokuden. It became clear that he wouldn't be satisfied until he saw a demonstration of this swordless swordsmanship. Bokuden asked the ferryman to steer over to a sandbar, where they could dock and engage in a duel.

When the boat reached the sandbar, the impetuous bully, intent on proving his prowess, jumped out and made way for level ground. Bokuden grabbed an oar and pushed the boat back into the lake and on course, leaving the second samurai behind. Bokuden shouted to him, "There you have it. An example of the techniques of the *Mutekatsu Ryu!*"

Rather than engaging in combat, Bokuden defeated the enemy with creativity. There's no reason to engage in conflict when you have options: *Thus, I say victory can be achieved. For even if the enemy is numerically stronger, we can prevent him from fighting.*

If you're good at what you do, have the quiet confidence to think creatively and come up with nontraditional solutions.

Nurture Subordinates

Former Macy's executive Sue Kronick valued the relationships she built and the people she helped during her career. "My sense is that I was making a difference to both the business and the people. You cannot imagine how rewarding that is," she reflected at her retirement. "When I'm lying on my death bed, I will not remember whether I was two, three or four percent ahead of plan. I will remember the people who I helped train and grow over the years."

This same compassion is shared by Carly Fiorina. After being unceremoniously ousted from HP, she reflected, "My heart ached that I was not given an opportunity to say good-bye to the people of HP, whom I had grown to love."

You may identify with some or all of these traits. These are comparative strengths many women possess. Study them and study yourself to understand how you can put your attributes to use for maximum benefit.

Failure Is a Fixed Point in Time

Do you know people who work hard—even around the clock—but have little to show for it? The paradox is that this hectic, always-moving pace makes it impossible to stop and evaluate what's working and what's not. These people plow through, hoping hard work and luck will plot their course to success. Sometimes it works. But hard work alone is rarely enough.

One of the hardest, most disillusioning lessons of my life was in learning that my hard work wasn't enough to prevent failure. When I began training in martial arts, I trained in "hard styles." This means when a powerful force comes, you are to meet it on its own terms, stop it, then inflict your own powerful force. But it didn't matter how frequently I trained, how many hours I spent trying to get stronger, and how many extra classes I squeezed out of my instructors. It didn't matter how many books I read, seminars I attended, or videos I studied. I couldn't stop the big guys who came in full force. And I sure couldn't dole out comparable force.

It wasn't fair. I felt like giving up, like I just didn't have what it took. I was easy to overpower. I often found myself bulldozed and dropped on the hard floor by an opponent who was stronger, but far less skilled.

Step Back and Evaluate

Everyone fails, but not everyone learns from it. Ultimately, I learned a lot from these mistakes. I learned that the theory of stopping a much stronger, much larger person's force, and then inflicting my own, wasn't going to work for me.

The idea of confronting force head-on was like a compact car colliding with an SUV. The compact car doesn't really have a chance, no matter how much it practices crashing into the SUV. This led me into martial arts that were better suited to deal with larger and stronger attackers.

Sometimes it's not how determined you are, how early you make it into the office, how long you've gone without a vacation, or how hard you work. It's not how many years you've been doing something. It's the end result. To win in the end, you need to step back from the everyday details. This takes examining the overarching paradigm to see if it truly fits with your nature and the reality of your goals. Is the way you're approaching the problem going to help you reach your objectives, or will it be a lesson in futility?

Companies go out of business all the time. Good people lose their jobs. It's not always because the owners and their people don't work hard enough. Sometimes you need to examine the problem and your approach to solving it. Recognizing that you need a course change, even a drastic course change, isn't failure. Hitting a powerful force head-on, like a compact car, most assuredly is.

Flow Like Water

Victory is in understanding and harnessing the landscape. It's in technique, finesse, execution, and understanding your enemy. It's also in your fluidity and ability to adapt. Sun Tzu says: *Now, the laws of military operations are like water. The tendency of water is to flow from heights to lowlands. The law of successful operations is to avoid the enemy's strength and strike his weaknesses. Water changes its course in accordance with the contours of the land. The soldier works out his victory in accordance with the situation of the enemy.*

Water just is. It's fluid and evasive. It's calm when it should be and mighty when it needs to be. It's nourishing and it's destructive. Like water, apply your strengths and attributes to achieve maximum result with minimum effort. That's the spirit behind powerfully successful business strategy.

BATTLEFIELD CHALLENGE

1. Which elements of Sun Tzu's science resonate with you? Which is easiest for you to apply and which is most difficult? Think of practical ways you can put his battlefield attributes into practice.

2. Think about a time when you've used better technique and altered the course in your favor. Identify specific reasons why this worked.

3. What have you learned from your professional failures? Think of five important lessons. More important, identify how you've applied what you're learned from those failures.

WOMAN WARRIOR

Drew Gilpin Faust Restores
Consensus Building at Harvard

In 2007, amid widespread controversy, Harvard University named Drew Gilpin Faust its first female president. This announcement was even more poignant coming on the heels of statements made by former president Lawrence H. Summers, who suggested that a lack of intrinsic ability is the reason why fewer women excel in math, engineering, and science in American universities.

A daughter of privilege, Faust was raised to be a rich man's wife. She had frequent confrontations with her mother, who told her, "It's a man's world, sweetie, and the sooner you learn that the better off you'll be."

Faust's presidency marks an opening of opportunities that she said "would have been inconceivable even a generation ago." Patricia Albjerg Graham, history of education professor emerita at Harvard, recalled in a *New York Times* article that as a postdoctoral fellow in 1972, she wasn't allowed to enter the main door of the faculty club or eat in the main dining room. The same article quoted Mary Waters, acting chairwoman of the sociology department, as saying, "It's been a lonely place for women, very lonely. There aren't many of us."

While Faust had no experience as a university president, her leadership style was instrumental in her selection. Summers had turned to her to help calm the reaction to his remarks about women's abilities, and to oversee two committees to help recruit, retain, and promote women in those fields at Harvard.

Faust's collaborative approach and people skills are well known among her peers. The former president, by contrast, had been accused of having an abrasive, confrontational style. Positioned to restore trust, Faust has successfully managed conflict and built strong allegiances, central principles of Sun Tzu.

"Faculty turned to her constantly as someone whose opinion is to be trusted," said Sheldon Hackney, a colleague and former president of the University of Pennsylvania. "She's very clear, well-organized. She has a sense of humor, but she's very even-keeled. You come to trust in her because she's so solid."

Wanting more for herself than to be a rich man's wife, today Faust is president of the most powerful university in the world.

Chapter 5

Self-Confidence

Our deepest fear is not that we are inadequate. Our deepest fear is that we are powerful beyond measure. It is our light, not our darkness, that frightens us. We ask ourselves, Who am I to be brilliant, gorgeous, talented, fabulous? Actually, who are you not to be?
—MARIANNE WILLIAMSON

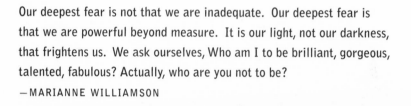

THE BATTLE: Too many women lack the confidence they need to be highly successful. If you're prone to second-guessing yourself, you'll reveal your insecurity.

THE CHAMPION: Boldly confident and self-assured, you are doubly powerful. You appear to be able to conquer anything. Then you do.

Fundamental to Sun Tzu's battlefield philosophy is self-belief. He says: *It follows that a triumphant army will not fight with the enemy until the victory is assured.* Self-confidence is a make-or-break attribute. To win big, you'll need to take the lessons from Sun Tzu and others to heart and apply them to your life. Sun Tzu writes about how the warrior-leader should lead. He is silent about the journey along the way.

But leaders don't just happen. They're forged in trial, error, and painful lessons. Belief in yourself determines how you'll make your journey.

Confidence Consequences

The average woman has more difficulty than the average man in believing she deserves more than she's offered. A core reason for this is lack of confidence, which carries over into all aspects of her career, not just her salary and bonuses. Many women hesitate to take the initiative to get what they want. "What's the point? I probably don't really deserve it after all," they rationalize.

The effects of poor self-confidence extend further than you may think. If you lack confidence in yourself, you're inadvertently spotlighting your weaknesses to everyone around you who's paying attention. If you suffer from a crisis of confidence, you won't reach your full potential and you won't inspire others: *When the general speaks in meek and subservient tone to his subordinates, he has lost the support of his men.*

But women who are confident and self-assured embody a key Sun Tzu concept of certain triumph: *It is a doctrine of war that we must not rely on the likelihood of the enemy not coming, but on our own readiness to meet him; not on the chance of his not attacking, but on the fact that we have made our position invincible.*

Embody Self-Confidence

According to Sun Tzu, you either believe in yourself or you don't. The general who lacks self-belief isn't fit to lead anyone. Sun Tzu has much to say about the qualities that influence self-confidence: boldness, decisiveness, commitment, authority, conviction, and right decision-making: *When campaigning, be swift as the wind; in leisurely march, be majestic as the forest; in raiding and plundering, be fierce as fire; in standing, be firm as the mountains. When hiding be as unfathomable as things behind the clouds; when moving, fall like a thunderclap.*

Confidence isn't innate. It's something you obtain. The best business warriors are the most secure and self-assured women. Those who are aware of their own abilities and those of their teams are the most successful, enjoy the most longevity, and feel the greatest sense of accomplishment.

Being confident in yourself and your abilities also encourages trust among your professional teams and everyone you touch. You carry this power into all other aspects of your life. This energy is part of who you are, and it's palpable to everyone around you.

When the Chihenne-Chiricahua Apache warrior Lozen fought for her people's freedom, she demonstrated belief in herself. This compelled the people to trust her, even though men were usually the only warriors.

In the 1870s, many of her people were forcibly moved to the San Carlos Reservation in Arizona. To protect her people's freedom, Lozen fought beside male warriors, rampaging against those who had taken their homeland. Many accounts tell us of her bravery and exceptional skill in combat.

Lozen inspired terrified women and children to cross the violent Rio Grande. One of the boys in that party later reported, "I saw a magnificent woman on a beautiful black horse—Lozen, the woman warrior! High above her head she held her rifle. There was a glitter as her right foot lifted and struck the shoulder of her horse." The women and children followed Lozen, trusting her implicitly. With her people safely across, she continued to battle. She later fought alongside Geronimo after his breakout from the reservation.

Burn the Boat

In desperate ground, fight a last-ditch battle.

If you possess self-belief, you're willing to do what it takes to achieve your dreams and reach your goals. For Sun Tzu, this worldview is fundamental to launching fierce campaigns and winning tremendous victories.

An example is Tariq ibn Ziyad, known in Spanish history as Taric the One-Eyed. He led the conquest of modern-day Spain. In the eighth century, upon landing with his men at Gibraltar, he ordered the ships that carried them to be burned. He declared to his soldiers, "Oh my warriors! There is nowhere to run away! The sea is behind you, and the enemy in front of you." His armies won decisively. This technique isn't unique to Tariq. Almost a millennium earlier, the Chinese general Xiang Yu ordered all his boats to be sunk, leaving his men with food for only three days. With winning or dying their only options, Xiang's troops conquered a vast area.

Roman generals were also known to set fire to their boats and bridges so the men couldn't use them for retreat. Each of these leaders sent a very clear message to the enemy. Their armies would not be defeated, no matter what.

Sun Tzu supports taking actions that will cause your people to give their very best: *Throw your soldiers into a position whence there is no escape, and they will choose death over desertion. For if prepared to die, how can the officers and men not exert their uttermost strength to fight? In a desperate situation, they fear nothing; when there is no way out, they stand firm. Deep in a hostile land they are bound together.*

Surrender Isn't an Option

These battlefield accounts can teach you a lot about yourself. Is your will to win, or the prize you stand to gain, so great that you're willing to burn the boat? Are you so committed you're willing to be the first to cross the torrents? With an indomitable spirit, are you willing to say: "I *can* do this. I *will* do this. No matter the adversity, I will risk it all to achieve tremendous success"?

If you're an entrepreneur, this means not giving in or quickly ditching your plans when things get tough. Giving in means lacking that absolute focus you need to be victorious. If easy retreat is an option, tremendous victory will never be.

An example is Johanna, a seasoned professional who had been trying to run and grow her small professional services company for years, while continuing to retreat to the safety of her day job. She realized she wasn't achieving the success she sought in either venture. Finally seeing that she couldn't dedicate herself completely to both, Johanna prepared to burn the boat and commit to her own business venture. Sometimes, crossing the torrent is the only way to get to the other side.

Measure Your Risks

Burning the boat doesn't mean taking uncalculated risks. Sun Tzu urges pragmatism: *The enlightened ruler is prudent, and the good general is full of caution. Thus, the state is kept secure and the army preserved.*

We all know people who've taken risks, only to fail. Sometimes if we retrace their steps, it's easy to see why they fell short. But burning the boat so you'll fight harder and ensure victory is an entirely different matter. It's wanting something achievable, and knowing you have the skills, will, and resources to achieve it. If you calculate well and you can burn the boat and cross the violent torrents, you have what it takes to triumph.

Gain Respect from the Inside Out (No Fairy Dust Needed)

When former Lucent chief and General Motors board member Pat Russo looks back on her career, she acknowledges that respect began on the inside. Earlier in her journey, when Russo was a marketing rep for IBM, a client refused to work with her because of her gender. But instead of needing external affirmation, Russo's philosophy was simple: "Don't talk a lot about it; just perform. Your record speaks for itself . . . I wish there was some magic there, but there's really no fairy dust."

Armed with self-belief, Russo has stepped boldly into positions of authority throughout her career. Refusing to allow others to jeopardize her self-belief or success, she assumed command in every instance and demonstrated that her vision was worth following. With each experience, she grew into her responsibilities and her abilities.

Like Russo, if you respect yourself first, the respect of others will follow. And in the case of those who wouldn't work with the female marketing rep, their respect really doesn't matter.

Timing Is Critical

Sun Tzu emphasizes repeatedly that timing is critical in every battle. Understanding and utilizing this to your advantage is fundamental. While you can foster your path to self-belief, you can't artificially force it. My own experience in the martial arts illustrates this point. Particularly around tests for advancements in rank, I didn't feel "ready." I missed that ethereal quality of confidence or legitimacy.

I did all that I could to prepare for these promotions. I spent countless hours getting ready. From cardio to training with partners, weight training, and following restrictive diets that would boost my performance, I took preparation seriously. But still, before, during, and after these tests, I felt as if I had just squeaked by.

Everything Changes

No one day or single event shifted this attitude. But the skills I accumulated over the years began to synergize. It happened from the inside out. My self-doubt slowly diminished.

What caused this shift in attitude? I wish I could neatly package it, but it was no single event. It was a process that came from time and dedication; from watching my peers and measuring myself against them; from studying less advanced students and perceiving the stark comparison. Ultimately, it came from arriving at confidence in myself.

Looking back, I realize quite simply that I wasn't ready until I was ready. In preparing my body, mind, and spirit daily, I began to accept that I'd given my all. I started to internalize the principles of what I studied rather than continuing to try to tack these principles onto my exterior. These principles and their execution became who I was.

This sort of self-acceptance occurs when you've worked for and sought it earnestly. It happens when you're ready, and not a moment before. It can't be decoded. It just is. No fairy dust required. If you believe in yourself and demand excellence at every turn, you'll grow into who you are to become. And you'll do it right on time.

Leave Your Comfort Zone

Nobody ever achieves anything by being comfortable . . . except comfort. But that quickly gets old if you're ambitious. If you don't stretch yourself and confront challenges, you won't grow.

Sun Tzu understands what it means to leave his comfort zone, and to lead his men far outside of theirs. His was a life of conflict. Forged in his battlefield experiences, Sun Tzu recognizes it takes leaving the comfort zone to bring out the best in people. Understand this and it will change how you regard conflicts in your life.

He writes: *To assemble the host of his army and bring it into danger—this may be termed the business of the general.*

Elaine Sarsynski, chairman and CEO of MassMutual International, understands that women need to break out of familiar territory. Working in financial services, she realizes it's rare for women to achieve top positions. For many women it's scary and risky to try something new. "That's why I encourage young women coming into this industry to do things that take them out of their comfort zone. By exploring different roles, women can discover new abilities they never knew they had, and all resulting experiences—good or bad—provide a platform for the next step up the ladder," she says. For Sarsynski, as for Sun Tzu, it's about stretching the boundaries of who you are to become who you'll be.

Enter the Pain Zone

I met my martial arts mentor, Uche Anusionwu, while we were undergraduates at Temple University in Philadelphia. When we met, I had been training for several years and was proud of my achievements. Uche, however, had been training hard from a very young age.

He had practiced *The Art of War* before I had ever heard of it. His take-no-prisoners approach was to get in and then disrupt, confuse, and destroy. My training to that point had more boundaries and more rules. I was completely overrun by Uche.

I tried to view these sessions as necessary to improving. However, I didn't get better every session. Sometimes I just got beaten up.

I remember one session in the foyer of my dorm room. A cold, institutional room, it was a tight twelve by twelve feet space. We didn't have any protective sparring gear. We didn't fight full contact, but we made good contact. Whenever we'd spar, I'd always come away bruised, scratched, and dinged. I was used to it. This day was no exception.

When you're losing the fight, and then losing your will to fight, you can feel the pain more vividly. Every thud and lasting hum of every bruised shin, forearm, and knuckle echoes. The sting of every busted lip lingers. Each shot that gets through, some in rapid succession, reminds you that you're losing. The painful sensation radiates deep beyond the flesh and stays fresh in the mind, limiting the desire to launch a proactive response. But when you're winning—or at least holding your own—adrenaline and enthusiasm mask the pain.

Uche feinted and set me up for a blazingly fast hip throw. I anticipated being dropped upper back-, neck- and head-first on the hard, tile floor. The intensity of the execution of the technique and my fear of bodily harm combined as I let out a solitary gasping sob of fear. The impact was negated as he followed through and caught me as I fell. But the fear and anticipation was anything but soft. I was defeated, for what felt like the twentieth time that day.

Comfort Is a Choice

I was tempted to stop training with this person who was so proficient at beating me. After all, if I didn't train with him, I wouldn't be reminded of my glaring weaknesses. We all feel better about ourselves when we aren't immobilized on our posterior, literally or metaphorically. Or, I could continue, find out what I needed to do to even the odds, and grow. I chose option number two.

After working with Uche for several years, I noticed a marked improvement. I was more aggressive, less fearful, more confident in myself, and better able to execute. Had I not left my comfort zone, I wouldn't have made the achievements I made in the years since. Today, I'd still be following a formulaic, predictable paradigm that didn't prepare me for the realities of combat. While the earlier days were tough, the impact these sessions had on my abilities and my confidence is beyond measure.

Yes, by leaving your comfort zone, you'll get knocked down and banged up, but it beats standing still. The sacrifices may be great, but well worth it.

BATTLEFIELD CHALLENGE

1. What's missing from your life that's keeping you from obtaining the confidence you need?
2. Identify the three most self-confident (yet not arrogant) people you know. How do you know they're filled with self-belief? Identify the three people in your business life who appear to be the least confident. What about them says they lack self-belief?
3. List the five most comfortable things about your current position, whether you're a mid-tier manager or running board meetings. In

what ways are these comforts good and in what ways do they keep you from excelling? How will moving beyond your comfort zone boost your performance?

4. Reaching goals builds confidence. Choose a focus area each year and set an ambitious goal. If your challenge is to become proficient in sales, study top sales books, attend seminars, talk with experts in your network, find a mentor, put what you learn into practice, and set sales goals. What will you focus on this year?

WOMAN WARRIOR

Condoleezza Rice:
Out of Struggle, Resilience

Condoleezza Rice, born in segregated Birmingham, Alabama, in 1954, grew up in a world that imposed limitations at every turn. But her family wouldn't buy into any of them. Her parents believed that the world their daughter would inhabit as an adult would afford greater opportunities. "My parents had me absolutely convinced that, well, you may not be able to have a hamburger at Woolworth's, but you could be president of the United States," she recalled.

Rice was instilled with a sense of self-worth that would take her to the White House, ultimately as secretary of state. General Colin Powell said of her upbringing, "She was raised in a protected environment to be a person of great self-confidence in Birmingham, where there was no reason to have self-confidence because you were a tenth-class citizen and you were black."

Her experiences as a child shaped the woman she'd become. She lived through the escalating violence of Birmingham in 1962 and 1963. Homes were attacked. Night Riders marauded through the community shooting, bombing, and setting fires to property owned by black people. A bomb killed four little black girls as they worshiped in church one Sunday morning. All of these experiences were meant to shatter spirits.

But rather than being knocked down by adversity, Rice applied the lessons. She said at the National Prayer Breakfast in 2003, "Only through struggle do we realize the depths of our resilience and understand that the hardest of blows can be survived and overcome." She believes that it's in struggle that men and women find redemption and arrive at the knowledge of who they are. "Struggle doesn't just strengthen us to survive hard times—it is also the key foundation for true optimism and accomplishment," said Rice.

Rice's path to diplomacy, and the White House, was atypical. The *Washington Post* noted her sometimes subtle advantage of being a beautiful woman in a male world of international politics and arms control. She didn't come from the military inside circle, nor did she follow the typical paths of Rhodes scholarship or the Brookings Institution. In fact, her biographer, Mary Beth Brown, has observed that Rice doesn't seek positions. She lets them find her. That doesn't happen without confidence.

Chapter 6

Focus

孫子

You have to master not only the art of listening to your head, you must also master listening to your heart and listening to your gut.
—CARLY FIORINA

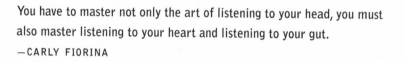

THE BATTLE: Focus is difficult in our fragmented, ten-things-at-once, deadline-driven culture. You frequently find yourself with too much to do to get anything done.

THE CHAMPION: You'll succeed when you can prioritize and zero in on problems to deliver sound and innovative solutions. This focus will come through in everything you do.

The speed and pressure some of us work under makes it difficult to focus on any one thing for more than a few hours or even minutes. The phone rings, the e-mail dings, a live human being walks into your office, the eleventh-hour project just changed course again . . . .

Focus to Get What You Want

Research indicates that men have a greater tendency to compartmentalize brain activity to focus on one task at a time. Women, however—as you may have noticed—are natural multitaskers. This can be an asset. But be careful not to allow a flurry of different and potentially competitive tasks and objectives to cause you to lose track of your real priorities.

For Sun Tzu, momentary lack of focus has dire consequences. It means the death of many of his men and even the fall of a state. A business culture that doesn't value focus, concerted effort, and fixed goals will also suffer disastrous ramifications. Excellence requires laser focus.

Carly Fiorina attributes focus to much of her success. Her advice to others: "Have an unflinching, clear-eyed vision of the goal, followed by absolute clarity, realism and objectivity about what it really will take to grow, to lead and to win," she said.

While serendipity should be exploited when it presents itself, success doesn't happen short of initiative and planning. Sun Tzu understands that single-mindedness is required to get what you want. And when it comes to people getting what they want, men have a far better handle on this than women do.

Landmark Negotiation Study

In *Women Don't Ask: Negotiation and the Gender Divide*, Linda Babcock and Sara Laschever report some illuminating findings on women's effectiveness in negotiations. Men, they found, ask for what they want twice as often as do women, and they open up negotiations four times as frequently. Women lose out because, as the title of the book implies, they simply don't ask. They don't ask for raises, promotions, better jobs, or recognition for their work. They don't ask for help at home. The authors sum this up as a reluctance to negotiate.

To reach this conclusion, Babcock evaluated salaries of Carnegie Mellon University students with graduate degrees. She found that the starting salaries of men were 7.6 percent higher—an average of $4,000 more—than the starting salaries of female graduates. She learned that only 7 percent of women negotiated, but a full 57 percent of men did!

This disparity also applies to women at the top. A 2008 Corporate Library survey of CEO pay at over 3,000 North American companies found that female CEOs earn only 85 percent of what male CEOs make. While women earn more in base pay, when cash bonuses, perks, and stock compensation were calculated, women come in a distant second.

Babcock and Laschever have some explanations for these stark contrasts. Women are far more inclined than men to worry about the impact that asking for more money and advancement will have on their relationships. They've determined that women fall into three categories:

1. We don't ask. After all, we don't want to be impolite.
2. We ask indirectly. Even though we may think our indirect, hint-hint approach gets through, it often falls flat with supervisors.
3. We commit to working harder so they'll see how deserving we are.

It's Not Just about Working Hard

Researchers and experts who've studied wage disparity have found that women often believe that if they work hard enough, everything will fall into place. After all, that's only fair. Unfortunately, it's a fallacy. This is examined in more detail in the Chapter 16: "Battlefield Widsom."

Different Sets of Rules

Another factor in why women don't ask is found in the way they're socialized. Their more structured form of play tends to teach compliance and rules, while boys are taught to push boundaries, be assertive, and make up their own rules.

I Don't Deserve It

Sometimes women aren't optimistic that they'll get what they want. Other times, they second-guess whether they actually deserve it.

Debra Condren, author of *Ambition Is Not A Dirty Word: A Woman's Guide to Earning Her Worth and Achieving Her Dreams*, believes that too much humility is a culprit. "Women are raised to believe that we're equally deserving and thinking that you're better than someone else— including that you've worked hard and should be paid well for the level of expertise you've achieved—is conceited," concludes Condren. This belief carries with it feelings of guilt and fear.

A Losing Scenario

These false beliefs have harmful consequences. They cause women to set less aggressive goals for themselves and settle for less than they're worth. Many women make modest initial offers and fold before they should. Male negotiators have been found to set goals about 15 percent higher than women in comparable situations. In fact, some researchers have concluded the wage gap could be eliminated if women just set goals comparable with men and committed to stick with them. This is not, however, a popularly held belief.

Condren makes another point that women should study carefully, especially those who are mothers. These same women may roll over when they should push for a better offer or a promotion. But when it comes to their children, they'll stop at nothing to see that their kids are treated fairly and get every advantage. They have what it takes to get what they want in the battles they believe in. That puts it in perspective, doesn't it?

Four Ways of Focus

To develop your focus, Sun Tzu urges the use of the following four methods: speed, depth, discipline, and seizing opportunities.

Act Quickly and Decisively

In directing such an enormous army, a speedy victory is the main object. If the war is long delayed, the men's weapons will be blunted and their ardor will be dampened.

This lesson is highlighted elsewhere in this book, and for good reason. It's important. To stay sharp, motivated, and ahead of your adversary, you need to act decisively to carry out your plan for victory. Sun Tzu warns about protracted military campaigns. They're costly in money, resources, and lives, and they're usually unsuccessful. To be a good steward of your personal and corporate resources, move quickly, attain victories, and keep moving forward.

Depth Is Required

Total commitment is necessary. The further you get into the campaign, the more cohesive your team will be, and the more difficult it will be to overcome its strength: *The deeper you penetrate into hostile territory, the greater will be the solidarity of your troops, and thus the defenders cannot overcome you. Generally, when invading a hostile territory, the deeper the troops penetrate, the more cohesive they will be; penetrating only a short way causes dispersion.*

You can apply this to the corporate, team, or individual level. To triumph over your greatest challenges, study deeply how you'll solve problems. A cosmetic strategy that only scratches the surface will fail. The deeper you are into the solution—the better you understand the landscape, yourself, and all of the battlefield conditions—the more likely you'll be to win. This solidarity of purpose is essential for Sun Tzu.

Disciplined Follow-Through

Ideas are ubiquitous. But follow-through requires focus and reliance. Whether you're a planner, an executor, or both, capitalizing on the momentum created in each victory is essential. Again, Sun Tzu says:

To win battles and capture lands and cities but fail to consolidate these achievements is ominous and may be described as a waste of resources and time. And, therefore, the enlightened ruler must deliberate upon the plans to go to battle and good generals carefully execute them.

If you aren't disciplined to follow through with your plans, you're wasting resources and time. This chaotic state can be seen in fragmented businesses without a clear direction, companies struggling with corporate identity, and companies run by individuals who aren't capable of defining or sticking to their long-term vision.

Miss No Opportunities along the Way

For Sun Tzu, winning requires grand plans and textbook execution. Persistent focus is required to avoid making mistakes. Skill and boldness in seizing opportunities is mandatory. These can be opportunities created by your opponent's mistakes, industry ebbs and flows, blazing innovations, serendipity, mergers and acquisitions, and a host of battlefield conditions. He says of the great general: *He wins his victories without making mistakes. Making no mistakes is what establishes the certainty of victory, for it means that he conquers an enemy already defeated. Accordingly, a wise commander always ensures that his forces are put in an invincible position, and at the same time will be sure to miss no opportunity to defeat the enemy.*

Get Out of the Sword's Way

Traditional Japanese swordsmanship is elegant, powerful, and deadly all at once. But gaining any level of skill requires considerable dedication and intensity. When you begin studying the sword, you use an *iaito*, a nonsharpened training sword. You spend many hours with this training weapon. You practice drawing, cutting the air, resheathing the blade, and drawing again. The most minute detail and angle will be practiced, studied, and improved upon. This practice is all in preparation to use a live, razor-sharp blade.

Using a sharp sword requires intense focus. The slightest miscalculation or lapse in concentration can result in serious injury. Because of this, using a sharp sword for the first time is petrifying. It's one of those heart-racing, pseudo-over-caffeinated sensations that reminds you you're alive.

This fear drives the focus of the practitioner. Every draw, every cut, every movement is done with unsurpassed concentration. Training with this absolute, unmitigated focus, you ultimately seek to become one with the sword. When it's in your hands, it's a sort of metaphysical connection.

The highest level of skill in Japanese swordsmanship is a complete paradox. When you begin training with this weapon, you're careful to be sure your digits and the rest of your body are out of the sword's way at all times. Then, after years of dedication, respect for the sword remains, but that initial fear is gone. Your focus and intention are refined. After fervent training, your goal is to get out of the sword's way so it can expertly and perfectly do what it was designed to do.

Get Out of Your Own Way

Like the expert swordsman, seek to focus on the task at hand and get out of your own way. Create the conditions for removing your barriers to success. These may be self-limiting beliefs, lack of training, inability to keep pace with technology, or the negative influence of others in your life. Overcome these and get them out of your way.

Begin by making sure you're not holding yourself back. You may have set a standard that keeps you from achieving. Or you may be underperforming based on the requirements of your current position or corporate culture. In both cases, you'll need to overcome these obstacles to reach your potential.

You must have the freedom to be unfettered by others, even superiors. This is one of the five points in which victory may be predicted for Sun Tzu: *He whose generals are able and not interfered with by the sovereign will win.*

Another land mine can be the people close to you. Even when you can't handpick each member of your team, you can be vigilant about the people you allow into your professional inner circle. Pick people who are positive, encouraging, and motivating. They don't all have to be big-shot, fast-track professionals. Not everyone with wisdom that will help you has an MBA, and not everyone with an MBA has wisdom. Surround yourself with people who are uplifting and trustworthy. Their counsel will help you get out of your own way.

Quiet!

How much solitude do you get during the course of the day? How much of that is time when you're fresh, alert, and creative? If you're like most people, the time that you get to yourself is only scraps, the crumbs of what's left after it's been used up by everyone and everything else. Women are natural collaborators and team builders. But no matter how much you value the team, you don't always need to be on the field with them. You need time to yourself, not just to rest and recharge, but also so you can create, innovate, and initiate.

Muriel Siebert was the first woman member of the New York Stock Exchange and founder of the brokerage Muriel Siebert & Co. She understands the value of quiet reflection. She advises, "Give yourself time to think. I used to take myself to a beach, with a pad of paper. It was a place where I could speak to myself."

Sun Tzu calls generals to make time to break away from the clutter of warfare: *It is the business of a general to be quiet and thus ensure depth in deliberation; impartial and upright, and thus keep a good management.*

Careful meditation is required to take the right action: *The different measures appropriate to the nine varieties of ground and the expediency of advance or withdrawal in accordance with circumstances and the fundamental laws of human nature are matters that must be studied carefully by a general.*

The lesson from Sun Tzu is not simply to think about solutions. Everyone does that. The lesson from Sun Tzu is to meditate deeply on serious issues and give yourself ample, unfettered time in quiet to reach conclusions. Deep reflection isn't a replacement for the value of your instincts. But you need enough quiet to hear from them.

Set Priorities

Carving out dedicated time for deep deliberation sounds easy enough. But carrying this out is a challenge for busy women. Guard your time and be true to the boundaries you set. There will always be people who want you to make an exception to serve their immediate needs. This is where your personal discipline, focus, and ability to say no come into play.

Joy Covey realized she needed extreme prioritization to manage her hectic schedule during the years of growth she presided over at Amazon. Her assistant scheduled her time in monthly themes. February, for example, was investor month. Covey's schedule reflected this focus. If it wasn't critical to the task that month and it wasn't on that monthly theme, it was pushed back.

Focus in Perspective

Focus is essential to getting what you want, realizing your potential, and staying on track to greatness. But let's put this all in perspective. This doesn't mean that if you don't follow every detail of a plan to the letter you're a failure. Changing course, shifting direction, and recalculating are all part of the fluidity and adaptation necessary to win your battles.

While Sun Tzu favors short battles that will end in victory, your life is a marathon. There will be times when you need to step back and recalibrate. This, too, is the deep deliberation called for by Sun Tzu.

Think Like an Olympian

Sometimes women who are naturally skilled at multitasking, but far less skilled in asking for help, take on too much. Scattered, they spend their days putting out fires and responding to emergencies. They don't get the opportunity to sit down and devote themselves meaningfully to their personal success.

Some entrepreneurs and small business leaders also attempt to do too much with too little. Possessing limited resources, they fail in setting their strategy to compete against much larger firms. They try to match them offering for offering to play at the big companies' level. Instead, they should concentrate their efforts. Dividing a larger enemy requires stealth, not duplicate tactics: *By exposing the enemy's dispositions and remaining invisible ourselves, we can keep our forces concentrated, while the enemy's must be divided.*

Concentrate your forces. With very rare exceptions, Olympic athletes don't compete in multiple sports. They don't even compete in every event in their sport. Not even Michael Phelps, the most decorated Olympian, competed in every men's swimming event in his monumental performance in the 2008 Beijing Games. Gold medalists and peak performers know they must dedicate their best efforts and focus where they can be successful. Follow their lead.

BATTLEFIELD CHALLENGE

1. Do you negotiate to get what you want? Do you set high goals and believe you deserve to get them? If you fail to get what you desire, to which pitfalls outlined here do you succumb? How has this chapter helped you ask for what you want?

2. Do you get enough quiet time to be effective? Identify the barriers in your lifestyle and work habits that keep you from the kind of reflection Sun Tzu advises. Use Siebert's example to identify a place where you can speak to—and hear—yourself.

3. What's in the way of your success? You may have self-limiting beliefs, lack of training, or waning motivation. Maybe you have negative influences or people who are greedy with your time. How can you get yourself and your obstacles out of the way of your success?

Marsha Serlin Defies the Odds with Laser Focus

When Marsha Serlin started United Scrap Metal, Inc., in 1978, she did it with $200 and a rented truck. She got into the industry because she noticed that a client in her former houseplant-installation business had a job that allowed him to be home a lot. With two small children she would soon be raising alone, flexibility was important. And with mounting debt from her husband's failed business, she needed a way to cover the bills and support her family. She had her client give her a crash course in scrap metal recycling. She then set about to do whatever it would take to grow the one-woman operation.

What it took was sixteen-hour days, six days a week. The seventh day was reserved for paperwork. So much for spending extra time with her children.

Serlin recalls repeatedly being underestimated in those early years. The scrap metal recycling business was no place for a lady, or so it seemed. Her competitors, all men, didn't expect her to survive. That was fine with her. "If you're underestimated, you have a real good chance to succeed. Nobody's watching, and you have an opportunity to go under the radar," reflected Serlin.

She maintained her focus and will to succeed. "I was the first woman to ever drive a truck and buy material and sell it," she said of her emergence onto the Chicago scrap metal scene. She got a lot of attention from the boys on the yard. "They would be in shock. They would watch me load the truck and stand in a circle and say. 'Watch that broad load all the steel!'" Load it she did, all by hand, just as they did. After the novelty wore off, the competition simply ignored her.

That, too, was fine with the entrepreneur. She was more than happy flying under the radar. She operated out of an old building reminiscent of the *Sanford and Son* TV show. She said the façade was intentional. With that exterior and the eyes of her competitors on the outside, she then bought up all the property behind her to clandestinely grow the business.

What began with a ramshackle old building, and an unlikely, yet fiercely focused and committed founder, has turned into an American success story. United Scrap processes 140,000 tons of steel a year and achieved a record $215 million in revenues in a recent year.

Chapter 7

Conquering Fear

邛子

Avoiding danger is no safer in the long run than outright exposure.
Life is either a daring adventure, or nothing.
—HELEN KELLER

> **THE BATTLE:** If you allow fear to dominate your decision making, you won't make much of the opportunities you receive.
>
> **THE CHAMPION:** Understand and harness fear, and it will motivate you forward. Refuse to allow it to hold you back and you'll be rewarded for the risks you take.

What impact has fear had in your career journey? For some, it has devastating consequences. For women who allow it to reign, a sad reality one day comes. They look back at the moves they didn't make because of fear and realize how much it has cost.

The Challenge of Fear

Renowned business and military minds have studied fear and its impact on us. *Think and Grow Rich* author Napoleon Hill puts it succinctly when he says, "Fear is the greatest obstacle to success." Whether you choose to blast through it, climb over it, or succumb to it, fear stands repeatedly in your path throughout your life. It threatens to keep you from happiness and achievement. Fear can make you long for safety and security. But to win, you must leverage adversity and overcome the fear it carries with it. In business, the kind of heart-pounding fear that accompanies conflict, tumult, risk, and transition is necessary for personal and corporate growth.

Fear is a basic survival mechanism that surrounds stressful and painful events, and threats of danger and pain. To overcome both its threats and realities, fear must be understood. A veteran of a lifetime of battles, Sun Tzu was well-acquainted with the conquest of fear—the fear of danger, failure, and death. Just as for Sun Tzu, your response to fear will have a profound influence on whether or not you realize your full potential. Sun Tzu says: *Only those who understand the dangers inherent in employing troops know how to conduct war in the most profitable way.*

Fear is a deeply motivating factor. Sun Tzu tells us leaders should use fear to overcome situations of great danger and turn it to our benefit: *Throw them into a perilous situation and they will survive; put them in desperate ground and they will live. For when the army is placed in such a situation, it can snatch victory from defeat.*

Today Is a Good Day to Die

You can adopt a resilient attitude of overcoming fear by internalizing the immortal words of the Lakota leader Crazy Horse. Going into battle, he inspired his people by shouting, "Today is a good day to die!"

These words reveal the spirit of a warrior. They speak to his confidence and peace with his abilities. Having trained well throughout his life, and having prepared his mind and body, he was ready to fight to the end with all he had. He wouldn't allow fear to define his response. This is an attitude of absolute peace over a situation and with yourself, no matter what the outcome.

Conquering fear doesn't mean no longer being afraid. It means controlling how you respond. For Sun Tzu, danger is simply a by-product of moving forward to win the battle: *Thus, both advantage and danger are inherent in maneuvering for an advantageous position.*

Growth requires occupying frightening and even dangerous positions. In times of danger, Sun Tzu knows warriors will be in a state of fear. The leader has prepared them well and carefully evaluated battlefield conditions. Their duty is only to carry out their purpose and to fight.

It's Not Fight or Flight, It's Tend and Befriend

Relatively recent studies on responses to stress provide insight into how women handle fear. Scientists Shelley Taylor and Laura Klein have uncovered a significant propensity for what they call "tend and befriend." When women face stress, the hormone oxytocin is released, producing a calming effect. It also promotes caretaking and social bonding. So, say Taylor and Klein, the release of oxytocin into women's bloodstreams blocks the typical fight-or-flight response (which is common in men) and prompts women to reach out for social support. The release of oxytocin doesn't have the same effect on men.

Understand, then, that it may be essential that you build support networks to help you through times of stress and fear. This doesn't mean you have to enter therapy. (But if you need to, no judgment here.) It does mean you probably need at least one trusted confidant.

Sun Tzu knew the importance of camaraderie. He writes about the spirit of soldiers serving together in hostile territory: *The deeper you penetrate into hostile territory, the greater will be the solidarity of your troops, and thus the defenses cannot overcome you.*

Conquer Fear with Preparation

Preparation is essential to Sun Tzu and harnessing fear begins with mental preparation. Have you reached the place in your journey where you can step back and say, "I'm ready for whatever comes next. I will meet it and triumph over it. I have worked hard and arrived at a state of proficiency"? That doesn't mean you stop getting better, but for today, you're fully prepared and ready for what may come.

Or should you have spent your time better? Maybe you should have called together fewer dead-end staff meetings and prepared your team for more high-value sales meetings. Or maybe you should have spent less time at happy hours and more time meaningfully networking. Should you have passed some tasks on to others so you could focus on tracking the competition? Or should you have spent more time empowering your people, and less time micromanaging them?

"Should-haves" are painful. You can't be resigned to win at all costs, and fight to the end if you're regretting that you didn't spend your yesterdays better. Reaching the mental and spiritual level of "today is a good day to die" requires honesty. It demands understanding where you want to go, and dedication to preparation in getting there.

That almost insurmountable battle may come tomorrow. Are you ready? According to Sun Tzu, once you and the people you lead are prepared and skilled, courage comes from channeling and overcoming fear: *On the day the army is ordered out to battle, your soldiers may weep, those sitting up wetting their garments, and those lying down letting the tears run down their cheeks. But throw them into a situation where there is no escape and they will display the immortal courage of Zhuan Zhu and Cao Kuei.*

This liberating state neutralizes the power fear can have over you.

Know Your Risks

Brigadier General Rhonda Cornum, PhD, MD, handled colossal fear and uncertainty as a prisoner of war in Iraq. Before deploying, she knew being taken prisoner was a possibility and understood the risks. Allowing herself to accept the potential, she elevated her preparation. When the helicopter she was in crashed and she was taken prisoner, she wasn't in denial. Accepting the risks is the first step in conquering fear.

Having "No Mind"

In Japanese Zen, the state of *mushin*, or "no mind," is tantamount to turning off your brain, shutting out the clutter of what-if scenarios and canned responses. Mushin means entering an engagement fully prepared and with clear objectives.

If you're well-trained and strong in spirit, and have conquered your fears, you won't go into battle steeped in anxiety. You won't anticipate. While you should be as prepared as possible for the engagement, you can't allow your mind to race with every counterpoint. It's tempting, but don't mistake preparation with becoming so consumed with formulating thoughts and arguments that you miss the key points your teammates, clients, and adversaries are making. If you're fixated on how well you'll respond, you'll be unprepared for the attack or challenge that comes.

As Sun Tzu tells us, no matter how thorough your preparation, you'll never know every detail before every engagement: *These are the keys to victory for a strategist. However, it is impossible to formulate them in detail beforehand.*

A Play Played Seriously

The words of Lee, Bruce Lee's somewhat autobiographical character in the 1973 *Enter the Dragon*, speak volumes on the power of becoming one with your response:

TEACHER: I see your talents have gone beyond the mere physical level. Your skills are now at the point of spiritual insight. I have several questions. What is the highest technique you hope to achieve?

LEE: To have no technique.

TEACHER: Very good. What are your thoughts when facing an opponent?

LEE: There is no opponent.

TEACHER: And why is that?

LEE: Because the word "I" does not exist.

TEACHER: So, continue . . .

LEE: A good fight should be like a small play, but played seriously. A good martial artist does not become tense, but ready. Not thinking, yet not dreaming. Ready for whatever may come. When the opponent expands, I contract. When he contracts, I expand. And when there is an opportunity, I do not hit. It hits all by itself.

The business application is profound. The greater your skill level, the better able you are to simply respond. You're not distracted by the clamor of your own thoughts and counters.

You've seen this in your career. The less someone knows, the more they feel compelled to try and demonstrate how much they do know. Their head is cluttered with retorts and counters. But it's in listening where they fall short. They're willing to speak, often saying very little.

Think of a fighter who's worked hard to prepare for a match. But rather than freeing her mind and body to take the initiative when it's presented and respond in accordance with her opponent, her mind races throughout the fight. "If she kicks low, I'll maneuver this way. If she drops her hands, I'll throw a left cross," she thinks.

This is a losing strategy. When she's thinking about her opponent kicking low, she's unexpectedly hit high. She's lost before the battle begins. Like this fighter, if your mind is cluttered with how you'll respond, you'll never be able to launch an effective attack. You'll always be on the defensive. This is to your detriment because the offensive is the superior position. Sun Tzu's direction is to exploit the enemy's weakness with an unrelenting offense: *His offensive will be irresistible if he plunges into the enemy's weak points.*

In battlefields and in business, you must know your adversary, her record, and her strengths and weaknesses. You must prepare based on all of those data points. But when it's showtime and the action is under way, relax, and let "no mind" put your fear to rest. With a calm mind, play the play seriously and simply react.

BATTLEFIELD CHALLENGE

1. When did you allow fear to be a too-important factor in a decision you made? Would you react differently today?

2. Do you have an effective support network? Do you need to be more open to reaching out to trusted confidants? Remember, if you're not an important source of support for someone, don't be surprised if you're not getting the backing *you* need.

3. Are you one with your response? Or are you set on furthering your agenda and forcing your message during presentations, meetings, and negotiations? How can you help calmness to prevail over the clutter and better react?

Rhonda Cornum, a POW in Iraq

There have been fewer than one hundred female prisoners of war in U.S. history. Now a highly decorated brigadier general, Rhonda Cornum, PhD, MD, was one of them. Hers is a story of overcoming and conquering great fear. On February 27, 1991, she was a flight surgeon aboard a Blackhawk searching for a downed F-16 pilot. Her helicopter was shot down. Cornum was among three soldiers who survived the crash. With two broken arms, a broken finger, torn knee ligaments, an eye glued shut with blood, a gunshot wound in the back, and other injuries, she climbed out from under the wreckage.

While being transported in Iraqi custody, Cornum then experienced what she sarcastically calls "the famous sexual assault." Badly injured, she was in no condition to fight back. She said her biggest concern wasn't rape, but that Sgt. Troy Dunlap, who was also taken captive, might find out and get killed trying to defend her.

Cornum was held prisoner for eight days. Although she wasn't tortured, she never knew what the next day would hold. She overcame the fear of this ordeal, and others she'd experienced in her career, because she was prepared.

Cornum was mentally, physically, emotionally, and spiritually ready for the reality that she was going to war, could be taken prisoner, and could be mistreated. She saw her responsibility as staying alive until she was rescued.

Instead of being ensnared by fear, Cornum focused on what she could control. She gave Sgt. Dunlap rudimentary instructions for treating her broken arms until she could get professional treatment. She focused on working to raise her pain threshold, initiating physical therapy, and beginning to heal, instead of focusing on the specter of interrogation and torture. She disciplined herself to keep track of the days and time. She and the two Iraqi women who were her keepers began teaching each other their languages.

Because of her willingness to prepare herself for the risks she took, she was able to overcome her fear and survive her imprisonment. When she came home from Iraq, Cornum continued her distinguished military career.

Chapter 8

Innovation

孫子

No condition, no matter how permanent it seems, is immune to change.
—CONDOLEEZZA RICE

> **THE BATTLE:** Innovation, adaptation, and flexibility require boldness, confidence, and knowledge of yourself, your adversary, your team, and your battlefield conditions. Innovation never comes out of mediocrity.
>
> **THE CHAMPION:** By creating superior solutions, staying ahead of competitors, meeting the needs of your talent, and executing based on dynamic and fluid realities, you'll succeed in ways not possible when you play by the rules.

Warriors who are victorious, and who live to fight their next battles, are quite often innovative. Innovation is requisite for survival. Those who can't change as conditions require lose out to those who can. Had Sun Tzu not survived battle after battle, whether by outright victory, evasion, or circumvention, he wouldn't have lived to share *The Art of War*.

Women-owned businesses are adapting to change, as evidenced by their survival and growth rate. For three decades, women have been starting businesses at twice the rate of men. Even more interesting, the growth and employment rates of these enterprises have outpaced the economy.

Innovation often occurs out of necessity. Female-fronted businesses get only 5 percent of venture capital, so from the very beginning, they must approach problems differently if they are to survive and thrive.

Sun Tzu on Innovation

Consider the potential of stealth and flexibility for microbusinesses, start-ups, and small businesses competing against well-established corporations—not to mention large businesses shifting into new territory. For armies of all sizes, Sun Tzu repeatedly calls for flexibility and maneuverability: *One who sets the entire army in motion with impedimenta to pursue an advantageous position will be too slow to attain it. If he abandons the camp and all the impedimenta to contend for advantage, the barrage and stores will be lost.*

In other words, large armies can be compromised by virtue of their size. If your adversary is better-funded, larger, and stronger than you are, instead of trying to fight battles on its terms, fight them on yours—where flexibility is advantageous.

Sun Tzu warns that leaders must adapt to battlefield conditions, not set upon a fixed and rigid methodology. He tells of one of the three ways a sovereign can bring damage to his army: *By interfering with direction of fighting, while ignorant of the military principle of adaption to circumstances. This sows doubts and misgivings in the minds of his officers and soldiers.*

Just as you shouldn't try to model male behavior to be successful as a woman, innovative and agile businesses shouldn't fall into the trap of emulating their larger rivals. You can't succeed based on their terms.

Regardless of whether you're the 600-pound gorilla in your industry or you're trying to unseat an entire jungle, flexibility to adapt to real circumstances is mandatory: *Be flexible and decide your line of action according to the situation on the enemy side.*

To be innovative is to hide your objectives from your competitors: *He shifts his campsites and undertakes marches by devious routes so as to make it impossible for others to anticipate his objective.*

Innovation Means Fluidity

For Sun Tzu, success calls for much more than tactics. It requires applying those tactics to a dynamic, fluid reality. This is a critical—and elusive—concept: *Even though we show people the victory gained by using flexible tactics in conformity to the changing situations, they do not comprehend this. People all know the tactics by which we achieved victory, but they do not know how the tactics were applied in the situation to defeat the enemy. Hence no victory is gained in the same manner as another. The tactics change in an infinite variety of ways to suit changes in the circumstances.*

Sun Tzu repeatedly urges wise generals to model water in how they adapt to circumstances: *Now, the laws of military operations are like water. . . . Water changes its course in accordance with the contours of the land. The soldier works out his victory in accordance with the situation of the enemy.*

The general who adapts well to battlefield circumstances also knows how to put people to best use: *The general who thoroughly understands the advantages that accompany variation of tactics knows how to employ troops. The general who does not is unable to use the terrain to his advantage even though he is well acquainted with it.*

Innovation Requires Preparation

Innovation is forged in preparation and foresight, and in knowing what the enemy has done and what he will do. Innovation is most powerful when it's least unexpected. Sun Tzu says: *Take advantage of the enemy's unpreparedness, make your way by unexpected routes, and attack him where he has taken no precautions.*

Perception in Innovation

Innovation that creates business results comes out of a sophisticated understanding of your situation. It's steeped in knowing your environment and what you're up against. This kind of 360-degree awareness is essential: *Weigh the situation before you move. He who knows the artifice of deviation will be victorious. Such is the art of maneuvering.*

Even if you're an agent of change, be perceptive to what's going on around you or you'll be caught off guard. As Carly Fiorina recalls: "What I wish I had understood at the outset—and I clearly didn't—is how much of a symbol of change everything about me was. Everything about me was a challenge to some people, and I don't think I understood that."

Apply perception when studying the enemy and watch for indicators of change. Trust your experience and your instincts: *When the enemy is close at hand and remains quiet, he is relying on favorable position. When he challenges battle from afar, he wishes to lure you to advance.... The rising of birds in their flight is the sign of an ambuscade. Startled beasts indicate that a sudden attack is forthcoming.*

Perception is born in knowledge. Here, Sun Tzu talks about the advantage of competitive intelligence—in this case, spies: *To foresee a victory no better than ordinary people's foresight is not the acme of excellence.*

Seizing Opportunities in Change

Conditions within certain industries have made them better suited for success for women. For companies and industries going through rapid change, growth, or turnaround, the status quo norms don't exist. Nontraditional ideas are sought. These often provide opportunities for women.

Fiorina emphasizes this principle when she tells the story of her days at AT&T. AT&T had been through a divestiture and the company, she says, was in a shambles. The Access Management division was in the worst shape. She says, "I decided that's where I wanted to work. People thought I was nuts. Nobody knows what they're doing, people said. It's a mess. And that's exactly what appealed to me. It was a wonderful challenge. I knew I could have a big impact, for better or for worse." She turned that division around, and learned the lessons she'd need to apply to turn around HP.

As CFO of Amazon, Joy Covey also looked at problems in new ways. With Amazon a new and unproven model, a lot of her team's time was spent thinking through problems in nontraditional ways. But with companies like Amazon came new opportunities. "What I think is very true of the tech world is that it's easy for talented people—whatever their gender, age, or race—to rise up and succeed," said Covey.

Indra Nooyi was drawn to PepsiCo because it was in a state of flux. While the food and beverage company is more traditional than telecom and technology, Nooyi was attracted to PepsiCo because she wanted to make a difference in a company that was struggling.

Sun Tzu is a proponent of discarding customs and convention when it's beneficial to winning. Here he advises on nontraditional ways of rewarding people and issuing orders: *Bestow rewards irrespective of customary practice and issue orders irrespective of convention and you can command a whole army as though it were but one man.*

Expect Change—Especially When It's Unexpected

Sun Tzu appreciates that nothing lasts forever and fluidity is essential: *There are neither fixed postures nor constant tactics in warfare. He who can modify his tactics in accordance with the enemy situation and thereby succeeds in winning may be said to be divine. Of the five elements, none is ever predominant; of the four seasons, none lasts forever; of the days, some are longer and others shorter; and of the moon, it sometimes waxes and sometimes wanes.*

Victory often goes to the person or organization that can better adapt, or innovate. Condoleezza Rice reminds us that nothing is beyond change. Of Christmas Eve 1991, she said, "On that night, the hammer and sickle, the flag of the mighty Soviet empire came down from above the Kremlin for the last time. You will be reminded that no condition, no matter how permanent it seems, is immune to change."

The experiences of world kickboxing champion Kathy Long taught her the same lesson about the unexpected. Echoing a sentiment similar to Rice's, with a somewhat different word choice, Long says, "On any given day anybody can get their ass kicked. No matter how good they are. Anybody."

Take Sun Tzu's lessons to heart to protect your posterior.

Move On from Mistakes

A man of ideals and absolutes, Sun Tzu calls for perfection. He has little regard for mistakes: *He wins his victories without making mistakes. Making no mistakes is what establishes the certainty of victory, for it means that he conquers an enemy already defeated.*

Making no mistakes, is, of course, an impossibility. But Sun Tzu's direction provides an opportunity to discuss some very interesting gender differences in how men and women view mistakes.

In *How Men Think*, Adrienne Mendell notes the different reactions of men and women regarding their mistakes. Women, in general, have a more difficult time when they make mistakes. She says this is because women are socialized to feel differently about mistakes. Boys are raised to be respected by their team if they learn from what they did wrong. Mistakes provide an opportunity to do better next time.

But for girls, it's different. When girls make mistakes, they're consoled. This reinforces the idea that they should feel badly about the mistakes. Mendell compared two partners in an architectural firm who made a mistake on a contract. The woman was devastated and wanted to give up for the rest of the day. The male partner wasn't ready to give in. He believed that even though the problem was severe, it could be solved. He worked through the night, resolved the issue, and they got the contract. The bottom line, said Mendell, is that women not only focus on mistakes, but often draw greater attention to them than is necessary. Men are more inclined to forget them and move on or fix them. Which trait do you exhibit?

Innovate by Pushing Boundaries

In your world, there are boundaries. You may even be restricted by the rules you set for yourself. As detailed in Chapter 3: "The Quest for Excellence," some women fall into self-limiting behavior and play too much within boundaries. Of course, there are institutional bounds and political plays you must understand. Ultimately, however, you're responsible for setting your personal boundaries and achieving what you will in life.

Boundaries can stifle your creativity and keep you from your best. For some, the work day starts in the morning and ends at 5:00 P.M., 6:00 P.M., or later. But if you're more productive, creative, or inspired at 5:00 A.M., or midnight, doesn't it make business sense to do your work at that time? The current world economy is creating great opportunities for freelancers, consultants, and virtual businesses that understand the value of empowering people to work on the terms and within the bounds that enable them to perform at their best.

If you're responsible for setting the standard for your business, are you holding the team back with ineffective paradigms that won't prepare them for the battlefield, or are you challenging them to be prepared for whatever will come? Performing as expected, within a fixed scenario, against predictable challenges, not only fails to allow you to progress, it can even atrophy your skill. But it does something even more damaging. It teaches you to play by rules that others won't respect.

As Sun Tzu says, *Keep the army moving and devise unfathomable plans.* If you follow the same fixed patterns day in and day out, your plans will be eminently fathomable. Think differently. Mix it up. Push the boundaries.

Fiorina agrees that adaptation is a mandatory growth strategy. But, it's not easy to introduce to a culture. "If you want to change the results of a business, you have to change how people operate, what they are doing, why they are doing it and what inspires them to do something differently," says Fiorina. "And so if you want, for example, to accelerate the rate of innovation in the business you have to think about how you get people to do something differently."

Innovation can be painful, but it doesn't hurt nearly as much as defeat.

BATTLEFIELD CHALLENGE

1. How do you deal with mistakes? Do you stop and dwell on them, or attempt to fix them if possible and move on if not possible?

2. What rules are you following that are keeping you from achieving? What boundaries, self-imposed or imposed by those around you, are keeping you from awesome success? What can you do to shake up these limitations?

3. Are you perceptive to the indicators of change that appear around you? How can you actively seek to discern what may lie ahead so you can seize those opportunities?

Joy Covey's Innovation at Amazon

Joy Covey was flying to an early morning analyst meeting for Amazon
.com when it dawned on her something was missing. She had left her
dress shoes on the plane. She needed a solution—and fast. She quickly
scanned well-dressed women in the baggage claim area of the airport.
Then she saw an acceptable pair worn by a woman who appeared to share
her shoe size, or close enough. Covey offered the woman $120 in cash
for the shoes on her feet. The woman refused, but was willing to sell her
another pair from her suitcase. Problem solved.

That's the kind of quick adaptation to circumstances that Sun
Tzu demands. It's also the kind of problem solving that defined an
extremely successful career for Covey as CFO for the still-young and
unproven Amazon. Covey took Amazon public and increased its value
exponentially. She then went on to serve as chief strategy officer for the
Internet company.

Raised in San Mateo, California, Covey didn't follow a conventional
path. She dropped out of high school at 16, though she later received
an equivalency diploma. At nineteen, she graduated from Fresno State
University with the second-highest score in the nation on the accounting
exam. She went on to earn joint degrees in business and law from
Harvard.

When she joined Amazon in 1996, it had a scant 150 employees and
$16 million in sales. Five months after her arrival, they raised company
revenue to $55 million and her personal value skyrocketed.

Covey looked at problems in new ways. The company routinely faced situations it had never seen because of its blazingly innovative business model. "Rather than asking ourselves, 'How has this been done in the past? What's the answer to this question?' we said, 'Where do we want to go and what are our goals?'" Her team spent a lot of time thinking through problems in ways that were nontraditional, but based on its core corporate principles.

Under her leadership, Amazon sacrificed short-term profits in favor of stable, long-term value. She and her team were committed to building a sustainable company. "So we asked ourselves," she recalls, "'how do we structure our conversations with Wall Street from the very beginning, before we even go public?'"

After all, innovation isn't worth much if the solutions it creates aren't enduring.

Chapter 9

Duty

孫子

One life is all we have and we live it as we believe in living it.
But to sacrifice what you are and to live without belief,
that is a fate more terrible than dying.
—JOAN OF ARC

> **THE BATTLE:** The fragmentation caused by scattered and competing priorities compromises success. By chasing the fairy tale of balancing a full-time home life and an around-the-clock work life, you're setting yourself up for failure at both.
>
> **THE CHAMPION:** Doing what you love and working in the best interest of the people who depend on you is the spirit and ethos of Sun Tzu. You're driven and ambitious while being realistic with expectations.

Sun Tzu sets the example he wants his people to follow. A right sense of duty is second nature to this general. To not fulfill his duty and not carry out his work is to not exist. It simply is who he is. Women who do the work they do because *it is who they are* understand this. Their work is a manifestation of their commitment to themselves and the lives they touch. The most successful women focus on much more than the bottom line.

They think about how to serve in the best interest of everyone who depends on them—employees, boards of directors, partners, clients, and families.

To take this duty seriously, you must continue to stay motivated and excel, regardless of what goes on around you. Whether it's mentoring, teaching, sharing, or simply listening, you'll carry out your responsibilities by honoring those who taught you and by respecting those who help you win. It's up to you to live out your duty, make excellence happen, and be a source of positivity in the lives of others.

Compassionate when needed and fierce when required, Sun Tzu has much to say about duty and responsibility.

Put Yourself First

Most women are intrinsically sensitive to the needs of others. But successful women understand they need to put themselves first so they can best lead, follow, and serve those in their professional and personal lives. No matter how many competing priorities you have each day, you're ultimately accountable for your successes and failures.

Always Be Learning

As detailed more fully in Chapter 17: "Continuous Learning" you have a duty to always better yourself. This means not staying in the same position for too long without being challenged and growing. It's not up to your boss or your board to challenge you and make you better today than you were yesterday. It's up to you. For Sun Tzu, complacency leads to loss of life and loss of way of life. On a different scale, it can be tragic for you too.

Putting yourself first has major implications for how seriously you take your personal growth and development. If you desire to be a powerful leader, but aren't seeking continuous self-improvement, you can't expect to stay on top for long.

Honor Your Boundaries

Set boundaries in your professional life so that you can have a rich personal life. Former Macy's executive Sue Kronick says women have told her that she showed them they could be very successful at work while living a balanced life. For example, she was always home for dinner on Friday nights. For Kronick, duty was about keeping the important commitments she made—both professional and personal.

Kronick points out that businesses, in this case, retail, have to adapt to people's needs and boundaries. "One of the things that the industry has to be careful of is that there are a lot of talented women that have children and can't be traveling all the time. They [businesses] also can't afford to lose those talented women. Businesses have to get creative and move talented women sometimes more laterally while their kids are growing up so they have cross-functional experience that may not involve traveling." Women should never feel like they're compromising their careers by going to their boss with concerns about their work's influence on their family responsibilities. For Kronick, successful professionals can be ambitious about family *and* career.

When Brenda Barnes ran PepsiCo, she worked seventy-hour weeks. Nevertheless, she set boundaries around her home life. Weekends were dedicated completely to family, at least as far as they knew. Any work she did Saturday or Sunday mornings was done while they were sleeping.

She also respected boundaries in leadership. "I never, ever call anyone on weekends. I never call meetings at very early hours, and I do my darnedest not to have them be late at night because I don't think it's my right to interfere with people's lives in that way."

Be Who You Are Always

Many women business owners equate their life's purpose with their business's purpose. For them, theirs is serious business that touches those around them. It's frequently these businesses that provide the ingredients that studies say will build enthusiastic, committed employees—equity, achievement, and camaraderie.

A major characteristic of women-owned businesses is the centrality of values. From her interviews with many women and her own personal experiences, Margaret Heffernan has concluded that women entrepreneurs are overwhelmingly less motivated by ego and money and more by serving others, namely employees and partners.

For these women, the purpose behind the business tightly equates with their deeply held values. They talk about their companies as living beings. These leaders see their role as teaching, nurturing, and otherwise living out their values. In many ways, they are mothers in their businesses. Heffernan sums it up this way: "Many women I know didn't start with a product idea or a service concept. They started with a philosophy, and that philosophy has guided them to their market."

Sun Tzu agrees that a general who fulfills a parental role for his troops will succeed. *If a general regards his men as infants, they will march with him into the deepest valleys. He treats them as his own beloved sons and they will stand by him unto death.*

Respect Rank

When Carly Fiorina arrived at HP, the organizational structure was flat. Business either got done by consensus or it didn't get done at all. She instilled a hierarchical structure that gave the executive council greater authority. Rank, competency, and performance were given renewed emphasis. This shift was instrumental in the company's transformation.

The Dangers of Not Respecting Rank

An effective chain of command is non-negotiable to Sun Tzu, and he repeatedly warns of the dangers of the alternative. The balance of the general's power hinges on enforcement of rank: *There are six situations that cause an army to fall. They are flight, insubordination, fall, collapse, disorganization, and rout. None of these disasters can be attributed to natural and geographical causes, but to the fault of the general.* This is the essence of those six situations:

1. In equal terrain, an army will flee from an attacking force ten times its size.
2. An army is insubordinate when the soldiers are strong and the officers are weak.
3. Even if the officers are valiant, if the soldiers are ineffective, then the army will fall.
4. If higher officers are looking after their own interests, instead of the army's, the army will collapse. Sun Tzu warns that this can happen when the commander-in-chief isn't aware of his officers' abilities.
5. If the general is incompetent, has little authority, mismanages his troops, allows a strained relationship between officers and men, or doesn't hold troops to high standards, the army will be disorganized.
6. If the general underestimates the enemy and fails to dedicate sufficient resources, the result is rout.

When any of these six situations exists, the army is on the road to defeat. It is the highest responsibility of the general that he examine them carefully.

When You Can't Respect Rank

Sun Tzu doesn't call for following orders at all costs. He realizes everyone has a choice: *If the sovereign heeds these stratagems of mine and acts upon them, he will surely win the war, and I shall, therefore, stay with him. If the sovereign neither heeds nor acts upon them, he will certainly suffer defeat, and I shall leave.*

Don't stay aboard a sinking ship when you have alternatives. You may feel powerless when you're in a less-than-ideal career position. But in reality, you have the freedom and the authority—even the responsibility—to make the changes necessary to realize your potential. Sun Tzu can choose to leave his sovereign. You can choose to leave a position, or even an employer.

Don't follow direction that you believe is misguided: *There are some roads which must not be followed, some troops which must not be attacked, some cities which must not be assaulted, some ground which must not be contested, and some commands of the sovereign which must not be obeyed.*

If you're an exceptional professional, you should never be in a position to follow orders that will lead to defeat: *If fighting does not stand a good chance of victory, you need not fight even though the sovereign has issued an order to engage.*

Be Realistic with Your People

Sun Tzu had a lot to say about how the general should care for and reward his men. Warfare is his way of life. He doesn't view it on a battle-by-battle basis. He knows he has to be a good steward of all the state's resources—not the least of whom are the men under his command. Sun Tzu is astutely aware of the dangers posed to an army stretched too thin.

To get the most out of the people under your command, you must use their skills without making demands that are too great: *A skilled commander sets great store by using the situation to the best advantage, and does not make excessive demands on his subordinates. Hence he is able to select the right men and exploits the situation. The energy of troops skillfully commanded is just like the momentum of round rocks quickly tumbling down from a mountain thousands of feet in height.*

Sun Tzu commands that you reward and tend to the complete needs of the people who report to you so they can perform at their best: *Plunder fertile country to supply your army with plentiful food. Pay attention to the soldiers' well-being and do not fatigue them. Try to keep them in high spirits and conserve their energy.*

Don't Exceed Your Grasp with Your Reach

It's easy to become fragmented with all of your responsibilities. Sometimes this is a product of leadership that follows what feels like a great idea today, then moves in the direction of the next great idea tomorrow. This expends energy and resources on activities that often don't fall under the company's strategic objectives. Trying to do too much with too little and forgetting what should drive corporate actions is a recipe for failure.

While his words don't all apply literally, Sun Tzu's ideas about fighting manageable wars are timeless: *When an army of one hundred thousand is raised and dispatched on a distant war, the expenses borne by the people together with the disbursements made by the treasury will amount to a thousand pieces of gold per day. There will be continuous commotion both at home and abroad; people will be involved with convoys and exhausted from performing transportation services, and seven hundred thousand households will be unable to continue their farmwork.*

Here, Sun Tzu is literally talking about waging a war across a wide geographic chasm. An application for you is to target a client base that allows you to be successful. If your sweet spot is the legal industry and universities, don't rapidly pursue manufacturers. If you're a lean organization with limited resources, don't expand your regional or domain focus into areas you can't physically support.

Dangers of Protracted Campaigns

In a passage replete with meaning and quoted elsewhere in this book, Sun Tzu warns of the consequences of battling too long: *In directing such an enormous army, a speedy victory is the main object. If the war is long delayed, the men's weapons will be blunted and their ardor will be dampened. If the army attacks cities, their strength will be exhausted.*

Your people can't keep up a breakneck pace over an extended period of time. They can't always do their best work during long and demanding hours that extend indefinitely. Their enthusiasm will wane and their drive and resources will be dulled.

Forced Marches

Sun Tzu counsels against pushing armies too hard for too long and too far beyond their means. Even the most skilled and enduring human beings have physical, mental, and emotional limitations. Sun Tzu recognizes this and knows that broken men are of no use. He urges realistic expectations: *When the army rolls up the armor and sets out speedily, stopping neither day nor night and marching at double speed for 100 li [30 miles] to wrest an advantage, the commander of three divisions will be captured. The vigorous troops will arrive first and the feeble will straggle along behind, so that if this method is used only one-tenth of the army will arrive. In a forced march of 50 li the commander of the first and van division will fall, and using this method but half of the army will arrive. In a forced march of 30 li, but two-thirds will arrive. Hence, the army will be lost without baggage train; and it cannot survive without provisions, nor can it last long without sources of supplies.*

People cannot be successful when the requirements are out of bounds and they don't have the resources to win. Sun Tzu knows never to take his people for granted and always to *pay attention to the soldiers' well-being.*

Elizabeth I followed this direction. Each summer she and her court traveled throughout the land. Despite the hardships, the queen knew this was important. She said, "We come for the hearts and allegiance of our subjects." She never took for granted that she had them. Like Sun

Tzu, Queen Elizabeth used caution in engaging her troops in battle and understood the great costs of war.

The lesson for you today is to nurture high performers and watch them—and your business—excel. Good people don't stick around in bad situations when too much is demanded and too little rewarded. This was just as true on the ancient battlefield as it is in executive suites and office cubicles today.

And Don't Force Yourself to March

Sun Tzu's call to be realistic with people isn't just about others. It applies to you as well. There are seasons in every ambitious woman's life where she has to work long, grueling hours. Young people beginning their careers, experienced women forging a new path, new entrepreneurs, leaders and others in times of crisis and transition, and those facing major milestones understand well the demands of these periods. The exhausting requirements come with the territory. The only way to meet the challenges faced in these scenarios is to put in the long hours necessary to prevail.

But what happens when that period becomes more than a time of transition? You're well established in your career, or making great progress to get there, and you're fighting daily to keep the pace. The norm is twelve- and fourteen-hour workdays, and weekends are for catching up on what you couldn't squeeze into the workweek. You haven't received so much as a "thank you" from anyone above your pay grade, and speaking of pay grade, that hasn't budged in quite a while either.

If your home life is suffering and there's no end in sight, if your career isn't progressing, the situation is tantamount to putting yourself through a forced march. You won't arrive at your destination fully intact.

Sun Tzu understands that resources are finite. Those resources include the spirit and stamina of people: *Again, if the army engages in protracted campaigns, the resources of the state will not suffice. Now, when your weapons are blunted, your ardor dampened, your strength exhausted and your treasure spent, neighboring rulers will take advantage of your distress to act. In this case, no man, however wise, is able to avert the disastrous consequences that ensue.*

He goes on: *A whole army may be robbed of its spirit, and its commander deprived of his presence of mind. Now, at the beginning of a campaign, the spirit of soldiers is keen; after a certain period of time, it declines; and in the later stage, it may be dwindled to naught.*

This condition creates weakness and fatigue that others can exploit. But if you're doing far too much for far too little, there's already a fair amount of exploitation going on.

If you're among the brave who've gone into business for yourself, you'll be marching very far for a very long time. Just remember to set a pace you can keep. Sun Tzu urges arriving at battles quickly—ahead of the enemy. He recognizes the importance of moving quickly and with great intensity. But he knows better than to require that of his men on a daily basis.

Shift the Balance

Identifying what matters to you is probably fairly simple. But living out your prioritization is likely a constant struggle. Maybe your faith is at the top of your priority list, but it's been so long since you've been to church that the last time you went everyone thought you were a first-time visitor. That's a priority problem. Your health is important, but your life is so chaotic that many of your meals come from drive-throughs. You haven't seen the inside of a gym in months and you're not sure where you put your running shoes. Something has to give.

Some women believe they have to be superwomen, until reality comes crashing down. Figuring out that your life is spinning out of control is easier for some than others. Changing that pattern and refining your habits is more difficult. To do this, identify the components of your career and your day that really matter and set boundaries to achieve the goals that are consistent with your values and the realistic demands of your life.

BATTLEFIELD CHALLENGE

1. Take an inventory of your professional gifts, from inherent abilities to beneficial relationships. Are you doing as much with these as you can? How could you better utilize these gifts and talents to improve yourself, your team, your organization, and all of the others who depend on you?

2. Define the responsibility you have to yourself. Then define your duty to the people who depend on you. In what ways are you fulfilling these requirements, and in what ways are you falling short? What will you do to improve your shortcomings?

3. What boundaries can you set and claim for yourself? In addition to those mentioned in this chapter, examples are completely taking Sundays off from work, not responding to e-mails after 7:00 P.M. any day, not missing your children's sports activities, and never canceling a date with your husband.

Brenda C. Barnes Retreats to Balance Career and Family

Brenda Barnes is best known as the woman who left the upper echelons of one *Fortune* 500 company to focus on family, only to go on to lead another corporate powerhouse when the time was right.

Barnes began her career at PepsiCo as a business manager for a division. One of few women, she experienced gender discrimination, but was determined to perform well and achieve her goal of becoming the head of sales. She proved good at achieving goals, ultimately becoming CEO of PepsiCo. She led her teams to strong sales and profits, and exceptional brand identity. Then, after twenty-two years with the company, she resigned, choosing to spend more time with her three young children and her husband.

For nine years, Barnes and her husband had lived in separate cities because of the extreme demands of their careers. Yet distance was just one sacrifice. She set her alarm for 3:30 A.M., and started her workday at home. At 7 A.M., she would wake her three children, with help from the nanny, and eat breakfast with them. Then it was off to the office until leaving for home at 7:00 P.M.

When Barnes left PepsiCo, she said, "I love what I do. But it's not a bad choice, to leave one thing you love to go to another thing you love." Pepsi tried to persuade her to stay by offering less-demanding responsibilities and a leave of absence, but Barnes was committed to her decision.

While she did leave to spend more time with her children (then ages seven, eight, and ten), she never took a complete break. During her hiatus, she served on seven corporate boards, became interim president of Starwood Hotels for a few months, and taught at the Kellogg Graduate School of Management.

Today she's president, CEO, and chairman of Sara Lee. She joined during a time of major transition. Sara Lee was embarking on a reorganization, which Barnes helped initiate. While the restructuring of the corporation was embraced on Wall Street, it wasn't exactly smooth. Sara Lee's stock prices dropped 23 percent during Barnes's first year as CEO. But once her influence was felt, profits were again on the rise in just over a year.

Her experience models Sun Tzu's call for retreating for the right reasons and acting in the best interest of the people and the organization: *The general that advances without coveting fame and retreats without fearing disgrace, whose only purpose is to protect his people and promote the best interest of his sovereign, is the precious jewel of the state.* She also exemplifies Sun Tzu's belief that when it's time to withdraw, it must be done quickly and with conviction: *He cannot be overtaken when he withdraws if he moves swiftly.*

Chapter 10

Authenticity

孫
子

Being powerful is like being a lady.
If you have to tell people you are, you aren't.
—MARGARET THATCHER

> **THE BATTLE:** The insecurity of limited self-belief will keep you from projecting your best and most genuine self.
>
> **THE CHAMPION:** When you're secure in yourself, you'll be consistent and genuine. You'll be a reliable leader and team member, up for any challenge you'll face.

Women who are secure in themselves and great at what they do are almost always genuine. Authentic businesswomen have no need to strive to be something they're not. Their achievements speak for themselves and their authenticity shows in all of their actions and interactions.

Authenticity is mandatory for Sun Tzu and for you. Self-doubt and second-guessing will undermine your ability to lead and execute. There are few things less impressive than a "leader" who fails to inspire confidence, and who lacks required characteristics like integrity, honesty, strength, and consistency.

Sun Tzu's great general's principles are fundamental to his authenticity: *The commander adept in war enhances the moral influence and adheres to the laws and regulations. Thus it is his power to control success.*

Overcome "Imposter Syndrome"

Unfortunately for many women, including highly successful achievers, the journey through their careers is filled with self-doubt, fear, and insecurity. In researching this phenomenon, now known as "Impostor Syndrome," Pauline Clance and Suzanne Imes studied 150 highly successful professional women. They found that even very accomplished women carry high levels of self-doubt that made them feel like, well, imposters.

While both men and women can be Imposter Syndrome victims, it's most often discussed in relation to women. If you suffer from this syndrome, each new achievement, rather than affirming your status, actually exacerbates your fear of being discovered as a fake. This deep lack of self-belief is naturally accompanied by an inability to internalize and reconcile successes.

If this describes you, you tend to believe you're getting by because of your contacts or because you've simply been lucky. Certainly, you believe, it's not because of your talent or skill. Imposter Syndrome goes far deeper than a normal case of self-doubt. Not only can it rob you of confidence and keep you from recognizing your achievements, it can also cause you to overwork to compensate for your perceived shortcomings.

There's no place for self-doubt for Sun Tzu. He commands decisiveness, preparation, and brilliance. Ultimately, it's about performance: *It is a doctrine of war that we must not rely on the likelihood of the enemy not coming, but on our own readiness to meet him; not on the chance of his not attacking, but on the fact that we have made our position invincible.*

Don't Lead Like He Does; Lead Like You Do

It's tempting for women who report primarily to men to believe they have to emulate men's management, leadership, and interpersonal styles. But you don't have to lead, or follow, like he does. You have to do it like you do. This means always being your authentic self.

Geraldine Laybourne, the co-founder and former chairman and CEO of Oxygen Media, sees simplicity in authenticity. For her, it's about being who you are—no matter what. She remembers seeing all the books in the 1980s about how women in the corporate world were supposed to act, dress, and talk. She said she never went down that look-alike path. "I just figured, You know what? I'm me. And I'm a much better me than anybody else. And if I try to be something I'm not, I'm not going to succeed. I can't be a man. I'm going to do a lousy job at being a man."

Sun Tzu says that leaders should have no conflict about what they're to do or who will believe in them. Act decisively, even in the most hostile scenarios, and people will follow you because of what you know, how you act, and who you are: *Therefore, when those experienced in war move, they are never bewildered; when they act, they are never at a loss. Thus the saying: Know the enemy and know yourself, and the victory will never be endangered; know the weather and know the ground, and your victory will then be complete.*

Respect Your Assets

By virtue of your gender, you will always be on the receiving end of others' expectations. Nina DiSesa, chairman and chief creative officer of McCann New York, notes that men aren't expected to be nurturing. But for women, nurturing is a foregone conclusion. DiSesa has seen women she's promoted abandon the nurturing tendencies that helped them on their climb up the ladder. But once they reach a top position, they stop working to earn their following. This causes them to lose the trust of their followers. Their genuine nature is called into question.

The Approval of Others

While collaboration can be an advantage, women who believe in themselves know when to rely on the opinions and advice of others, and when to go with their brains and instinct. Such independence has benefited many successful women. For Joy Covey, independence was forged in her experiences. After dropping out of high school, she took a job as a grocery clerk before deciding to get back on track. She earned her high school equivalency diploma and then finished college in two and a half years. Covey said those experiences shaped her into a woman who didn't require the approval of others to make tough choices. This has carried over into how she's made decisions throughout her career.

Show Authentic Strength

The practical application of this passage from Sun Tzu may not be immediately clear: *A master of war wins victories without showing his brilliant military success, and without gaining the reputation for wisdom or the merit for valor.*

To illuminate it, let's look at an example from a chapter in American diplomatic history. This episode, recounted in Mary Beth Brown's biography of Condoleezza Rice, *Condi: The Life of a Steel Magnolia*, occurs in 1989, late in the Cold War. Rice was thirty-four years old and working at the National Security Council in the White House. At the time, President George H. W. Bush wanted to encourage Boris Yeltsin's growing democratic movement in what was then the Soviet Union. But the president had to be careful not to offend his ally, the Soviet General Secretary Mikhail Gorbachev.

The United States conceived a plan to bring Yeltsin into the White House through the west basement to meet with National Security Advisor Brent Scowcroft. This would avoid media attention. President Bush would then drop in for an unofficial, impromptu meeting. Everyone would be happy.

The Russian leader arrived at the entrance. He was met by Rice, who was supposed to escort him to Scowcroft's office. But the plan wasn't agreeable to Yeltsin. He was used to getting what he wanted. He demanded a meeting with the president and wouldn't settle for anything less. About meeting with Scowcroft, Yeltsin said, "I've never heard of General Scowcroft. He's not important enough to meet with me." He demanded to meet with the president and told Rice that he wouldn't leave until she guaranteed him that he would.

According to Rice's biographer, the standoff and stare-down lasted about five minutes, with Yeltsin "infuriated" and Rice "resolute." That's a long time to be staring down a Russian leader during the Cold War. Rice ultimately began to turn away and advised that he return to his hotel. She'd let Scowcroft know there wouldn't be a meeting today.

"Then," writes Brown, "Yeltsin blinked. The duel was over. Yeltsin conceded, agreeing to meet with Scowcroft." Rice then escorted him to Scowcroft's office, President Bush dropped by for a few minutes, and Yeltsin was pleased. Rice was calm, controlled, and confident throughout the entire encounter.

This incident made an impression on White House aides and others. President Bush remarked later, "Condi was brilliant, but she never tried to flaunt it while in meetings with foreign leaders. . . . Her temperament was such that she had an amazing way of getting along with people, of making a strong point without being disagreeable to those who differed. . . . She has a manner and presence that disarms the biggest of big shots. Why? Because they know she knows what she is talking about."

That's how she was known for dealing with the most difficult foreign leaders. She didn't puff herself up or put on a display of false strength. She didn't need to feed her ego or pander to gain the favor of others. Rather, Rice was respected and achieved victories like this because she understood the challenges she faced and was equipped to meet them.

This is what Sun Tzu means in the passage that began this section. Boris Yeltsin didn't walk into that confrontation with a high regard for the brilliance, wisdom, and valor of the adversary he would face. He didn't know who or what he was up against. Rice's team, on the other hand, had calculated their plan well—and just as important, executed well. This passage, first mentioned in Chapter 6: "Focus," bears repeating: *Making no mistakes is what establishes the certainty of victory, for it means that he conquers an enemy already defeated.*

The Symbolic and the Real

When most people begin training in a martial art, they do it because they want to get a black belt. An emblem of a crowning achievement, this goal is one of the greatest motivational factors of all beginning-to-intermediate martial artists. In popular culture, it's synonymous with proficiency. A black belt separates the student from the expert, the proven from the masses.

As the day of the black belt exam approaches, it consumes more of the martial artist's waking thoughts than anything else—and a lot of her dreams. She oscillates between questioning her preparedness for the test and trying to assure herself that her time is now.

When she earns the belt, she feels tremendous accomplishment. At the end of this intense physical and psychological journey, she's on top of the world.

Now what? If it's a hard school, she goes home and recovers from a grueling exam. She nurses her wounds and sleeps the sound sleep of victory. She comes back for the next class two days later with that stiff new belt tied around her waist. She has a new lease on life and probably even carries herself differently beneath that new belt. Having proved herself before her instructors and her peers, she has a new confidence in what she can do.

Reality Check

But the reality is that the two days since her test didn't make any difference. She's not any more skilled wearing that piece of fabric than she was before she donned it. She's not a different person and she hasn't radically transformed her skill set. It won't take her long to realize that. When she does, she'll be disappointed. She may think she hasn't worked hard enough, that she has somehow unwittingly cheated the system. Like the women with Imposter Syndrome, she may think she's a fraud.

The new black belt isn't at fault. This is just part of the journey. She's learned a fundamental lesson about the value of symbols. If she walks out of that dojo door, goes home, and is attacked while in the parking lot of her apartment complex, the attacker doesn't attack her black belt. He doesn't attack the style of martial art she studies. He attacks *her*. The symbol won't help her. Only the reality will.

Just about everyone who reaches for new personal or professional challenges can relate to this at some point. You get a promotion, a challenging new job, take a risky career move, or make a major shift in the way you run your business. If you feel instantly empowered, as if your decision has bestowed magical new powers on you, you're kidding yourself. Reality will eventually set in.

Like the new black belt, we all have to grow into our achievements. The test isn't in whether or not you make it, but in how you live it out. Real, sustainable victory comes in believing in yourself. And with this comes others' belief in you.

The Big Picture

Who you are is bigger than the job you do and the title you have. Work is an aspect of your purpose, but you must always keep your focus on the big picture if you're going to realize the full potential life has for you. This focus on what matters has to remain at the forefront daily. To do this, you must be authentic. And if you're authentic, your life will reflect your passion.

Sun Tzu is talking about an army when he writes about a united purpose, but this can just as easily be applied to the struggles you face daily: *He whose ranks are united in purpose will win.*

For her book *Naked in the Boardroom*, Robin Wolaner talked to many trailblazing career women about their achievements. Each cited romance, family, and relationship milestones along the way, as well as educational achievements. Wolaner observes that women tend to see the big picture, even when talking about their career victories. She contrasts this with the few lines devoted to each of Jack Welch's marriages in *Straight from the Gut*, the autobiography of the former chairman and CEO of General Electric.

The point is not that men don't value family, relationships, and education. Of course they do. The point is that women feel that being true to themselves involves much more than what they do behind their desks and in board meetings.

If you're authentic, everyone will know it. If you're authentic and excellent, you'll be invaluable to an organization that's worthy of you. You will embody Sun Tzu's assessment: *The general who advances without coveting fame and retreats without fearing disgrace, whose only purpose is to protect his people and promote the best interests of his sovereign, is the precious jewel of the state.*

BATTLEFIELD CHALLENGE

1. In business or elsewhere in your life, think about times when you tried to be something you weren't to impress others or gain acceptance. What did that experience teach you? Why do you think you fell into it?

2. Think about an encounter you had that parallels that of Condoleezza Rice with Boris Yeltsin, when you were called to hold your ground. Were you victorious? Why or why not? What do Rice's experience and your personal experience teach you about projecting authentic strength?

3. Can you relate to Imposter Syndrome? If so, how has this chapter challenged you to overcome your persistent self-doubt? Write down all your daily victories—small and large—and go back and review them regularly. Regularly reinforce your attributes and your wins. Confide in and seek encouragement of trusted colleagues, and consider getting a mentor.

WOMAN WARRIOR

For Indra Nooyi, Being Powerful Means Being Herself

Indra Nooyi is reinventing PepsiCo, but she's not about to reinvent herself to do it.

The PepsiCo CEO first joined the corporation as its chief strategist. Her calculations have paid off for the beverage and food giant. Nooyi pushed for the spinoff of Taco Bell, Pizza Hut, and KFC. She directed the acquisition of Tropicana and the merger with Quaker Oats.

While what she's done and how she's done it are compelling business lessons, the woman behind the success is equally compelling. She has sought to embrace her unique characteristics, even in the corporate world. After beginning her career in India, she moved to the United States. She received her master's degree in public and private management from Yale. Then it was off to the job market. She interviewed with Boston Consulting Group, opting to wear a sari to the meeting. While this traditional attire would be more commonly seen in India than on American corporate floors, staying true to herself paid off. She was offered the job.

Comfort is important to Nooyi, who is at home in her own skin. She's been known to walk the halls at Pepsi barefoot, sometimes even singing along the way. Chief Executive Roger Enrico said, "Indra can drive as deep and hard as anyone I've ever met, but she can do it with a sense of heart and fun."

Nooyi was drawn to PepsiCo by the chance to make a difference in a struggling company. Since 2000, when she was named CFO, revenues have soared 72 percent and net profits more than doubled in a recent year. She's now boldly moving the brand into the realm of healthy food.

Nooyi is a picture of the American dream. She's been featured in the *Wall Street Journal*'s list of 50 Women to Watch two years running, was named to the TIME 100 list of the most influential people in the world for two years, and has been ranked by *Fortune* as the single most powerful woman in business.

Yes, Nooyi has made it. But she keeps track of what's important. "At the end of the day, don't forget that you're a person, don't forget you're a mother, don't forget you're a wife, don't forget you're a daughter," she urges. Because in the end, no matter how much money you make and how much success you create, "What you're left is family, friends, and faith."

Chapter 11

Harness Deception to Shape Perception

If you're underestimated, you have a real good chance to succeed. Nobody's watching, and you have an opportunity to go under the radar.
—MARSHA SERLIN

THE BATTLE: If you show your methods and intentions to your competitors, you'll lose clients, market share, employees, and opportunities along the way. You will prepare your adversary to defeat you.

THE CHAMPION: You'll have an advantage if you understand how to seize opportunities created by the real and false perceptions of others.

The idea of deception is complicated. It's also a practice that Sun Tzu thoroughly and unapologetically embraces. For him, deception is using any means necessary to accomplish his objectives. Sometimes deceptive tactics create confusion and chaos among the enemy's ranks. Other times they create a false understanding of a situation for the enemy. At all times, Sun Tzu seeks to shape perceptions to his advantage.

If you're not a fan of deceiving others to get what you want, this chapter still has lessons for you. Rather than focusing on deception, focus on ways you can take advantage of your opponent's confusion, false perceptions, or lack of understanding.

For some of the women highlighted in this chapter, deception is about getting out of the way of what others believe and using their misperceptions to an advantage. In the final analysis, the lesson is in understanding the importance of *perception*, despite the reality.

Sun Tzu's daily charge is to defend his troops, his people, and his state. To do this, he needs to use every tool and opportunity to his advantage, including deception. Remember, however, that Sun Tzu is a highly principled commander and advocates the same behavior for those who would study his words. He believes in leading his men with valor and following his sovereign's direction, if it's principled and effective. For Sun Tzu, leaders must exert ethical standards: *The commander adept in war enhances the moral influence and adheres to the laws and regulations. Thus it is in his power to control success.*

It's beyond the scope of this book to define your moral code for you. You must utilize deception, disorientation, and disruption within the confines of youself, your business, and your culture. However you choose to define these, Sun Tzu is instructive. And even if spreading lies about yourself and others isn't how you choose to do business, there are plenty of others who don't share those ethics. Sun Tzu's lessons on deception and perception can help you overtake adversaries who play by different rules.

Sun Tzu on Deception

Deception is a critical method of forcing the enemy to stay on the move: *Now, war is based on deception. Move when it is advantageous and change tactics by dispersal and concentration of your troops.*

Sun Tzu directs warrior-leaders to foster a disconnect between the way things *appear* to the enemy and the way things actually *are*. Keeping the enemy on the move and in a defensive state robs him of his advantage. It creates an opportunity for you: *One who is adept at keeping the enemy on the move maintains deceitful appearances, according to which the enemy will act. He lures with something that the enemy is certain to take. By so doing he keeps the enemy on the move and then waits for the right moment to make a sudden ambush with picked troops.*

Sun Tzu also advises generals of the importance of keeping their objectives unknown to the adversary. The path less traveled is unexpected by the enemy: *He changes his arrangements and alters his plans in order to make others unable to see through his strategies. He shifts his campsites and undertakes marches by devious routes so as to make it impossible for others to anticipate his objectives.*

The superior general should be enigmatic, and as Sun Tzu says, unfathomable.

Let Them Underestimate You

In Chapter 4: "Technique—Your Advantage," I discussed the attributes of exceptional leadership. These are timing; seizing opportunities; creating opportunities; speed; unleashing energy; and spirit. Sun Tzu directs that you combine these elements with manipulating the enemy's perception for great result. Keep the enemy uncertain and insecure, fixated on how he'll respond to you, instead of how he'll advance and overtake you. Or, if you're in a position of power, allow your enemy to be ill prepared in her overconfidence: *All warfare is based on deception. Therefore, when able to attack, we must pretend to be unable; when employing our forces, we must seem inactive; when we are near, we must make the enemy believe we are far away; when far away, we must make him believe we are near.*

Here are some examples of women who harnessed deception, disorientation, and disruption to manipulate battlefield factors in their favor, keep the opponent on the move, and make their plans incomprehensible to enemies.

Examples of Underestimation

Examples abound of great women in business and throughout history who have been underestimated because of factors such as gender, color, status, and lack of formal education.

Like Harriet Tubman, whose story was told in Chapter 2: "Indomitable Spirit," Mary Bowser pretended to be uneducated and illiterate. She was employed by Confederate President Jefferson Davis and worked in his home. The problem for Davis and the Confederacy was that Bowser wasn't illiterate. She read the papers on his desk and passed the details on to Union Army supporters.

Elizabeth I represents both sides of the perception equation. She needed to project power. The perception of a strong, vibrant queen was essential to convey to her friends and foes alike. The reality, however, was that she suffered many health issues throughout her life. Refusing to allow any sign of weakness compromise her reign, she consciously communicated strength. But, when she could use it to her advantage, Elizabeth allowed herself to be underestimated. She's known to have referred to herself as a "mere woman" or a "weak woman."

In the example of Marsha Serlin detailed in Chapter 6: "Focus," we have a case study in using the assumptions of others to your advantage.

Shape Perception to Your Advantage

Those stories are examples of shaping perception and using it as an advantage, or simply benefiting from false beliefs. Sun Tzu provides a great deal of advice on how generals should craft appearances, as well as how to make determinations about the appearances of the enemy: *When the enemy's envoys speak in humble terms, but the army continues preparations, that means it will advance. . . . When his troops march speedily and parade in formations, he is expecting to fight a decisive battle on a fixed date. When half his force advances and half retreats, he is attempting to decoy you. When his troops lean on their weapons, they are famished. . . . When the enemy sees an advantage but does not advance to seize it, he is fatigued.*

Study Sun Tzu's telltale signs of weakness and strength and adopt this for your business. Develop your own indicators to know when your adversary is going to advance and when it's going to retreat. Determine signs that will help you know when the enemy's resources are low and when they're plentiful. This knowledge will go a long way in helping you plan and time your attack. Study these factors well, weigh the data points, and trust your instincts so you don't fall into a deception trap your enemy may be laying for you.

Whenever possible, allow the enemy's perception be used to your own advantage. Let your enemy perceive you as weaker than you are. Sun Tzu advises that you wait to reveal your hand until such time as he'll be unable to put up a strong defense: *At first, then, exhibit the coyness of a maiden until the enemy gives you an opening; afterwards be swift as a running hare, and it will be too late for the enemy to oppose you.*

Then, after you have lured the enemy in by shaping perception, manipulating circumstances, or causing disorientation, be ready to launch your decisive attack: *That you are certain to take what you attack is because you attack a place the enemy does not or cannot protect.*

A Mystery to the Enemy

The victorious will operate under a shroud of mystery. For Sun Tzu, the ways of the triumphant will be imperceptible: *The spot where we intend to fight must not be made known. In this way, the enemy must take precautions at many places against the attack. The more places he must guard, the fewer his troops we shall have to face at any given point.*

By keeping your intentions and plans from your enemy, you can also be selective about the battles you will and won't fight: *If we do not wish to fight, we can prevent him from engaging us even though the lines of our encampment be merely traced out on the ground. This is because we divert him from going where he wishes.*

BATTLEFIELD CHALLENGE

1. Have you ever allowed being underestimated to work to your advantage? If it was successful, how can you replicate that to defeat the next enemy?

2. Are you effectively leveraging perception? Do you promote movements that should be stealth so transparently that your opponent can come directly for you? Or are you so quiet about your accomplishments that neither your opponent nor your best prospects or recruits are thinking of you? How can you best strike this balance?

3. Think about a time when you were strategically deceived by a competitor, team member, employee, partner, or colleague. Why was your adversary able to trick you? What did you learn to ensure you don't ever find yourself in a similar position?

WOMAN WARRIOR

Queen Nzinga:
A Case Study in Deception

Born in 1580 in modern-day Angola, West Africa, Nzinga lived in turbulent times. The Portuguese were invading and rapidly expanding their power with the Atlantic slave trade.

Highly regarded today for her intelligence and brilliant battlefield execution, she became queen at forty-two, following her father's reign. Her leadership is a case study in deception. She repeatedly tricked and misled the Portuguese. She had her troops pretend to be captured, then gather firearms, break free, and bring the guns back home. When her sister was taken prisoner, Nzinga used her as a source of intelligence for years until she was ultimately killed by her captors.

The queen formed alliances with Europeans, including the Dutch, to bolster her strength. She allowed her chief enemy to baptize her into Christianity in a show of alliance following the signing of a peace treaty. There are also accounts of her adoption of cannibalism to gain the respect of an influential—and certainly very brutal—tribe. These tales may or may not be true. It's possible they were created by the Portuguese to discredit her.

What's known without doubt is that Queen Nzinga was a fierce warrior. She frequently led her troops into battle. Among the successful strategies that would have received Sun Tzu's approval, she lured enemies further and further inland. The Europeans, who didn't expect this level of sophistication from an African queen, were at an even greater disadvantage when overcome with it.

A famous account of Nzinga at a peace treaty sums up her intensity, creativity, and indomitable spirit. The Portuguese were ready to negotiate the terms of peace, but wouldn't do it on equal footing. They had arranged just enough chairs for themselves, but none for her. Refusing to give ground, Nzinga turned to her attendants. One came forward and dropped to his hands and knees, fashioning a suitable chair. She demonstrated that she wouldn't back down. The treaty was signed then and there.

Nzinga died peacefully at eighty-two, resisting the enemy until the end. At her passing, the Portuguese increased their occupation of the region.

Chapter 12

Preparedness

Preparation, I have often said, is rightly two-thirds of any venture.
—AMELIA EARHART

> **THE BATTLE:** Success will elude you if you won't prepare for
> the reality of current and future circumstances. You'll repeat
> mistakes and always be ready to fall victim to new ones.
>
> **THE CHAMPION:** You're ready for change and unexpected
> consequences. If you're prepared, you'll be equipped to execute
> well. You'll come to every attack ready for that battle, even if
> it's an ambush.

Success in business and on the battlefield means always being ready
for the expected and the unexpected. You must be able to anticipate
in advance what will come, and, as Sun Tzu says, have "foreknowledge." Preparation is at the core of *The Art of War*. Without the ability to anticipate and be ready for attacks and create opportunities for
strong offenses, you won't be triumphant.

Even more basically, you need proper resources for each campaign.
Sun Tzu explains that the seasoned commander can anticipate resource

needs: *Those adept at employing troops do not require a second levy of conscripts or more than two provisionings. They carry military supplies from the homeland and make up for their provisions relying on the enemy. Thus the army will always be plentifully provided.*

Preparedness in Business

Genevieve Bos, publisher of *PINK* magazine, said preparation has been fundamental to her success. "Amazingly, I have never had problems with raising money or selling to clients because in my career I was prepared for the meetings. I did my homework and leveraged my virtual board of directors to help with business plans."

In difficult situations, your job and your business depend on your readiness for what lies ahead. Sun Tzu writes that if you've trained well and honestly assessed yourself, your adversary, and the conditions of battle, and you're ready, you can handle any encounter you'll face. Preparation is a defining factor in the outcome: *He who is well prepared and lies in wait for an enemy who is not well prepared will win.*

If you're serious about developing the kind of excellence personified by Sun Tzu, you need to always be in a state of readiness. Allow yourself to slip into complacency and your skills and your fortitude will atrophy. While you often can't control what happens to you, you can control how you respond. You alone can define how ready you are for the challenge. Your greatest battle may be tomorrow. Are you ready for it?

Anybody Can Take Out Anybody

Sun Tzu says to leverage your enemy's state of unpreparedness: *Take advantage of the enemy's unpreparedness, make your way by unexpected routes, and attack him where he has taken no precautions.*

"No, that's not going to get it. Come on! Look, it's like this. Punch!"

I threw yet another punch at my instructor as he grew increasingly angry and impatient.

Slam. He dropped me hard on my back, again. By this time I'd lost count of how many times I'd been slammed to the floor. The welt on my sternum throbbed just enough for me to know it was there. But it paled in comparison to my pride.

The instructor, who outweighed me by at least 100 pounds, was trying to get me to execute a simultaneous foot sweep and palm strike to the sternum to take him down. The moral of this story is not the poorly conceived nature of the technique I was being taught. It isn't the flawed approach that, if I simply used enough head-on force, I'd be able to take him down. But these are worth mentioning, because they show that even imperfect strategies can win—on occasion.

Each time I tried, I failed to take him down or so much as move him. We were both getting frustrated. He decided to slow the technique in one more attempt for me to get it. He punched slowly to allow me to close in and get my timing right.

I tried once more. This time, he dropped heavily to the mat. Success! I was stunned. But he was even more stunned. He just lay there quietly for quite a few seconds. Then he started to mutter through evident pain, "I wasn't ready. My knee . . . I wasn't . . . I didn't know you were . . . ." He looked like a turtle stuck on his shell, dazed, uncertain of what to do next. He tried to bend the rear leg that had been planted firmly before the takedown, but the slightest movement was clearly excruciating.

The class gathered around him quietly. No one knew how to respond or what to do. We waited, softly asking if we could do anything. Everyone was disoriented. After a few minutes, when he was ready, we helped him to a chair.

He got hurt badly because his attention was diverted. Otherwise, there was no way I could have done that technique effectively on him.

While I was focusing on what I was doing, he momentarily lost focus and the knee of his support leg gave out from under him.

This incident taught me that, if timing and resources are exploited, *anybody* can get the better of *anybody* on the right day. Though it wasn't my intent to hurt him, this was an unforgettable lesson in how much easier it is to take the big guy down when his attention is diverted.

The Shot You Don't Expect Will Take You Out

Preparation puts you in a better position than your opponent. It causes your adversary to have to adapt to keep up with you, rather than innovating to stay ahead of you: *Numerical weakness comes from having to prepare against possible attacks; numerical strength from compelling the enemy to make these preparations against us.*

Boxers will tell you that the punch that knocks them out is the one they don't see coming. If they can't parry or dodge the blows they see coming, they can at least anticipate and absorb them. Absorbing the punch allows them to mute the impact. But blows that sneak inside their periphery or that are set up so that the next punch is felt rather than seen are the ones that matter. Unexpected blows do the most damage.

An example of this came during a Friday evening class I was teaching. A visiting student, Surya, was an experienced martial artist. She was very small, about 120 pounds. The second student, Allen, was newer. He had been with me for about six months, and while he was by no means big, he had at least fifty pounds on her. They were working on a foot sweep. Coincidentally, it has similarities with the technique mentioned above. Only, this was my class, and the sweeps I teach are much more effective against larger people than the ones I'd learned years before.

Both students knew how to fall. When the sweep is done correctly, it can be a hard landing. But it's easy to absorb when you know how to hit the mat. You tuck your head, focus, exhale, and fall correctly.

Before we started the technique, I told them both not to underestimate the amount of force the other could generate. When you fail to fall properly from this sweep, your entire body regrets it.

Allen executed the technique first on Surya. His form was decent, and she was easy to take down. Then it was Surya's turn. While she had been rusty and hadn't trained for some months, she moved in expertly, broke his balance, thrust forward, and swept out his primary support leg. He hit the ground with a thud. The physical mechanics of his fall were in order. He tucked his head and slapped off to dissipate the amount of force he expected from her. But he had failed to prepare his body—and most important, his mind—to absorb the impact. He hadn't effectively focused the right muscles or controlled the amount of air pressed out of his diaphragm when he hit the ground. He got the wind knocked out of him pretty badly. He lay there for a few moments in silence, unable to move.

When he got his wind back, he groaned and slowly and clumsily got his feet under him. Allen did a quick mental body check to make sure everything was still where it was supposed to be. As he rose slowly and began to focus his eyes, he realized the force of the landing had knocked out one of his contacts. This was something I had never seen before, and have never seen since. Contacts come out all the time during sparring, but rarely with the impact of a throw, or more specifically, a landing.

When You Assume, You Land on Your . . .

Despite advance notice, Allen grossly underestimated the ability of his much smaller opponent to inflict damage. He paid for it. If this had been a combat scenario, after the fall stunned him, Surya would have followed up with any number of locks or blows as he lay virtually helpless on his back, trying to catch his breath. These few moments of confusion were all she would have needed to do mortal damage if the situation called for it. His mistake created the opportunity. He underestimated his opponent and made assumptions based on appearances.

If you're unprepared, your adversary creates an opportunity for you to overtake him. Be watchful to take advantage of these opportunities and be sure not to fall into them yourself. As Sun Tzu puts it: *If the enemy leaves a door open, you must rush in. Seize the place the enemy values without making an appointment to battle with him. Be flexible and decide your line of action according to the situation on the enemy side.*

Dangers of Generalization

Practically, we can all fall into the mistake of making gross generalizations about people based on our past experiences or even the size of our egos. Always remember that with each individual, you could be wrong. It's like a peer told me once when I'd reached a conclusion too soon about a mutual acquaintance: "If you don't have enough data points yet, I recommend you don't come to a conclusion." Good advice. Always be open to changing your mind—preferably before you land on your posterior and it's too late.

Imagine what would happen if you applied this lesson to people on your team. If you expect more out of them, there's a good chance you'll get more out of them. Expect the best and you just might get it. If you're underestimating good people, challenging these assumptions and giving them greater responsibility could enable them to break through the foolish boundaries you've built.

There's one more lesson from Allen and Surya. It's consistent with the concept and practice of zanshin, which is explained in Chapter 3: "The Quest for Excellence." Follow through with what you're doing, even if it's bigger than you are. In this case, Surya was fully aware of what she could accomplish, moved in, and executed a good technique with a solid follow-through. Even if a challenge is difficult, follow it through to completion. It's amazing what you'll be able to achieve if you trust yourself and seize opportunities.

Be Ready for the Worst-Case Scenario

While Sun Tzu cautions that only those battles that can be won and will advance your cause should be fought, he realizes that not all situations you'll find yourself in will be optimal. You can turn worst-case scenarios to your advantage, if you're prepared for them: *A wise general in his deliberations must consider both favorable and unfavorable factors. By taking into account the favorable factors, he makes his plan feasible; by taking into account the unfavorable, he may avoid disasters.*

Sun Tzu advocates for having so deeply prepared for even the worst outcomes as to have already lived through them and overcome them.

Brigadier General Rhonda Cornum was mentally reconciled to the very real possibility that she could become a prisoner of war in Iraq. On the business battlefield, Carly Fiorina repeatedly put herself into high-risk positions amidst great conflict and great opportunity. Muriel Siebert, who pioneered a career in the quintessential boys' club on Wall Street, said that preparing for the worst was always a factor in her business endeavors. "What are the best things that could happen, and what are the worst things? If I couldn't take the worst thing that could happen I wouldn't do it," she says.

These women and others profiled in this book are examples of *snatching victory from defeat.* With resilience and indomitable spirit, they turned desperate disadvantages to their favor. They were ready for the worst-case scenario. You must be, too.

Grasp the Essence

For legendary swordsman and samurai Miyamoto Musashi, knowing himself, his weapons, his surroundings, and the enemy were all as important as his physical skill in fighting battles. He was a master at preparedness. On many occasions, he fought highly skilled swordsmen to the death, choosing to use a long wooden staff against their razor-sharp swords. Despite bringing a stick to a swordfight, Musashi was eminently ready for every encounter. He never lost a battle.

Musashi is the picture of preparedness. He studied each challenge and knew what he was up against. He confused, disoriented, and frustrated his opponents, based on identifying their unique weaknesses. He frequently changed the rules of engagement, and assaulted his opponents' pride. In this way, he defeated them before the battle was under way. Regardless of the tactics Musashi employed, the root of his achievements was in his constant state of readiness.

The Heart of the Strategy

In *Samurai Strategies*, Boye Lafayette De Mente gets to the heart of Musashi's fighting strategy. "The message that he taught over and over again, and in myriad ways, was that unfailing success in fighting and in any other endeavor is based on not being blinded by illusions—by grasping the essence of one's self, one's opponents or competitors, the task at hand, the circumstances of the physical location, and the surrounding environment," he writes.

We don't usually think in terms of "grasping the essence" in the West. We may study something and gather as much data as we can, seeking to command an intellectual knowledge. In some ways, our research complicates the subject we examine, and understanding its essence becomes more elusive.

To really understand the challenges and opportunities you face, you must see things at their simplest. Online media pioneer Dany Levy expressed it like this: "Try to boil down what you're doing to one very simple idea. And ask a lot of questions. That's the nature of being an entrepreneur. It doesn't matter if you come from a farm or if you went to Harvard Business School. The fact is, you don't know jack until you're doing it." For Levy, Sun Tzu, and for you, preparation comes from understanding and immersion.

Beyond the Facts

Seeking to grasp the essence means much more than accumulating data. It's also about moving beyond the surface to understand the nature of what you're examining. Grasping the essence involves far more than logic. It demands perception, and it commands simplicity. Grasping the essence means achieving an intuitive, intrinsic understanding.

Indra Nooyi, CEO of PepsiCo, is a woman of bold vision. But more than a visionary, she's a focused leader. In moving the company from snack foods to healthy foods, she's grasped the essence of the mission. Her lofty goal, as she puts it, is to "bring together what is good for business with what is good for the world."

Ultimately, grasping the essence of something is understanding it at its most complex so its simplicity is fully revealed. You will see your challenge, enemy, team, and circumstances in their purest form. Preparation also requires you to examine and understand yourself in the same manner.

BATTLEFIELD CHALLENGE

1. Preparation calls for vigilant honing of skills and fresh evaluation. Are you training and thinking today as you did ten years ago, five years ago, or one year ago? Have you updated the challenges to include obstacles you may not have formerly conceived of or wanted to think of?

2. Do you put in the extra effort to understand your competition, industry, developments, and trends? Do you regularly train yourself with books, seminars, market research, and other tools? What should you do to be ready to seize opportunities and overcome even unforeseen challenges?

3. Think about five of the worst-case scenarios you could face in your career. These may be a bankruptcy, merger, or corporate restructuring. How can you best prepare for these possibilities today so you're ready to adapt and triumph tomorrow?

WOMAN WARRIOR

Sue Kronick,
Prepared to Create Opportunity

Sun Kronick spent nearly thirty-seven years at Macy's, formerly Federated Department Stores, Inc. She began her career there in 1973 as an executive trainee at Bloomingdale's. She rose up the ranks until retiring as vice chair, Department Store Divisions. She deeply understood how the organization worked, and throughout her career, created opportunities to climb the ranks.

Kronick climbed all the way to *Fortune*'s 25 Highest-Paid Women list. Her success strategies included creating opportunities, being prepared to seize them when the timing was right, and crafting execution to get results. Here's an example that spring-boarded her career and altered the course of her company.

Kronick was working as vice president and merchandising manager at Bloomingdale's. She had the good fortune of running into Howard Goldfeder, chairman and CEO of Federated. In a brief face-to-face conversation, Goldfeder asked her how things were going. He probably didn't expect the response he got. Kronick replied that she thought she could move faster. Ten days later she was offered a big promotion to general merchandise manager and senior vice president.

What sounds like a lucky break was a whole lot more. Kronick knew that Goldfeder would be in town. She was sure to be on the management floor for this well-timed "impromptu" meeting.

This is an example of living out the battlefield reality experienced by Sun Tzu, as translated by Philip Martin McCaulay: *Opportunities multiply as they are seized.*

The strategy of going above and beyond carried over to other facets of business for Kronick. Looking back, she believes a major part of the cultural imprint she left on Macy's was the example she set for building relationships inside the company and externally with suppliers. Macy's was committed to doing business the right way and with integrity. She made sure to live out those principles during her tenure.

Chapter 13

Understand Yourself

孫子

Don't compromise yourself. You are all you've got.
—JANIS JOPLIN

> **THE BATTLE:** Understanding yourself takes honesty, emotional maturity, and perspective. You must assess your strengths to maximize them. You must also diagnose and compensate for your weaknesses so you can defeat smart adversaries.
>
> **THE CHAMPION:** Knowing yourself and being comfortable in your skin gives you an advantage in understanding others, finding colleagues' and competitors' strengths and weaknesses, and communicating from a position of power. Skill in evaluating yourself will empower you to always make improvements.

For Sun Tzu, to be a successful strategist you must foremost be true to yourself. You must *know* yourself. You must be able to honestly and objectively evaluate yourself. This sounds easier than it is.

While many women are experts at understanding the needs and agendas of others, not everyone is able to get to the core of who and what they are. As discussed in Chapter 10: "Authenticity," being in tune with who you are is the only way to harness your potential on your path to who you can be.

You'll never truly be effective with any of the strategies or tactics you'll lay forth if you don't first understand yourself. The focus of this chapter is the individual, but certainly this applies just as readily to organizations.

Conquer Your Weaknesses

Although very successful, Geraldine Laybourne was smart enough to know she needed help. Rather than avoid her weaknesses and hope no one else noticed, she built a team that helped round them out. "I have a high tolerance for ambiguity," she said. "So I make sure I surround myself with people who have a high sense of urgency." Laybourne recognizes that acting decisively is important in business, and she builds strong teams to enable this.

International martial arts legend and film star Bruce Lee is an impeccable illustration of how to understand yourself and conquer weakness. Lee is often taken to be the picture of exceptional health, stamina, precision, and power. He's romanticized as perfection. But he wasn't, of course. His limitations included his size—he was short—his nearsightedness, and having one leg a full inch shorter than the other. He also suffered a serious injury as a young man that threatened to cripple him for life.

Confronting Limitations

Instead of avoiding his weaknesses, Lee acknowledged and reconciled them. He then dedicated his training to compensating for these shortcomings, while still maximizing his strengths. Lee understood that, like you, he wouldn't get far if he didn't reconcile himself to his limitations. They're a starting point.

He said his shorter left leg drove him to discover that the best fighting stance for him was with a right lead. This provided an advantage with some kicks and an uneven stomp that enabled greater momentum. His nearsightedness dictated he'd have to study a close-quarter combat system, so he began with the Chinese infighting style *wing chun.* "I accepted my limitations for what they were and capitalized on them. And that's what you must learn to do," he said.

Manipulate Circumstances to Overcome Weaknesses

Through his personal journey, Lee laid a foundation for a groundbreaking worldview that revolutionized martial arts. He promoted the idea that each individual should exploit strategies and tactics based on his or her own physical attributes.

In addition to identifying your attributes and liabilities—and even more importantly—Lee said you have to change the rules of the game. Manipulate circumstances so you can bring your assets to bear. Turn your weaknesses into strengths by changing the conditions. This is a page out of *The Art of War.*

Sun Tzu advises that manipulating circumstances to gain advantage is exceedingly difficult, but worth the effort: *During the process from assembling the troops and mobilizing the people to deploying the army ready for battle, nothing is more difficult than the art of maneuvering, for seizing favorable positions beforehand. What is difficult about it is to make the devious route the most direct and to turn disadvantage to advantage. Thus, forcing the enemy to deviate and slow down his march by luring him with a bait, you may set out after he does and arrive at the battlefield before him.*

Manipulate Circumstances to Overcome *Perceived* Weaknesses

Muriel Siebert never would have been successful by her terms if she played by the rules. She knew what it was like to be innovative in one of the most traditional old boys' clubs—Wall Street. Born in 1932, she was the first woman to own a seat on the New York Stock Exchange. To do this, she had to work from a position of disadvantage to manipulate circumstances in her favor.

"I bought a seat on the NYSE and started my own firm because I wanted to be paid equally," Siebert told *Smart Money* magazine. "I couldn't go to a large firm then—they didn't have women." She then asked a client, "'What large firm can I go to where I can get credit on the business that I'm doing?' He said, 'Don't be ridiculous, you won't. Buy a seat and work for yourself.'"

Changing the game is a smart tactic whether your goal is to dominate your industry, create a compelling new business model, or rise within your company. Some women go to great lengths to change their circumstances, including starting their own ventures. If you run a business, you have a lot of influence over the circumstances you create around you. The same can also be said for women in leadership who aren't entrepreneurs.

Victim of Circumstance

Not everyone wants to change the game. An extreme example is Sally, who runs her own consulting business. She repeatedly complains to anyone who will listen that her client and prospect base is the Department of Defense. The decision-makers are mostly men and they just don't give women opportunities. She has had a long line of doors closed in her face. She's sure it comes down to her gender.

If you met Sally and spent just a few moments with her, you'd probably be looking for a door to close on her, too. She's intent on making excuses for why her practice will never be successful, despite having a background in working with the Department of Defense. Surely, she knew of these perceived difficulties before she began a business predicated upon selling into that institution. Yet, she's opted to build a business based on a self-limiting certainty that she won't be successful.

Don't be a victim of battlefield conditions. Alter them to your advantage.

Accountability for Your Circumstances

Sally created the business. She set its rules. And she opted to play by established rules that she thought would always leave her defeated. What she didn't understand, but Lee, Laybourne, and so many other winners do, is that your success comes down to you. In the long game, failure is always an option if you allow it.

Regardless of your title, you're the general of your career destiny. Many professional women and men choose to ignore their weaknesses. Denial is easier than the hard work of getting better. It's so much easier to recognize and work to hone strengths. This denial mindset includes the false belief that others will ignore your weaknesses, too. But it doesn't work that way.

Your adversaries will exploit your weaknesses. Competitors will build products that surpass yours, and the market will know the difference. Peers you compete with will see where you're weak and seize opportunities to ensure they get the promotion and you don't. Outstanding recruits will choose to work for companies that have assessed their problem areas and are always working to improve. Companies and individuals who can't adapt to threats from superior technologies and tools will go the way of the dinosaurs. You can't afford not to diagnose and address your weaknesses.

If you're a smart, talented, and driven professional and you're not getting what you need from your career, company, or job, change your circumstances.

Strength Will Create Enemies

Traditionally, women have been socialized to avoid conflict. We're supposed to find nonaggressive, pleasant, unobtrusive solutions—or simply leave the matter unresolved. Politeness is more important than getting what you want.

Not surprisingly, this is in stark contrast to Sun Tzu's call to take decisive action: *In battle, a good commander creates a posture releasing an irresistible and overwhelming momentum, and his attack is precisely timed in a quick tempo.*

Sun Tzu calls for acting with boldness to put your assets into action. To achieve this, you'll need to make peace with the reality that being assertive and getting what you want means making some enemies. Don't set out to make enemies, but be ready for that consequence.

Your conviction and strength of character will threaten and even frighten some. The strong will push you even further and call you to demonstrate what you're made of. The weak will murmur and seek ways to undermine you. If you know you're in the right, don't take these dynamics to heart. Accept them as a matter of course. Recognize the source of others' lashing out for what it is, whether it's insecurity, fear, lack of information, or some other problem your adversaries have.

Don't Apologize for Your Strengths

An element of strength is confidence in yourself and your decisions. This requires overcoming the tendency many women have to be conciliatory or apologetic in the face of adversity. When others point a finger at you in assigning blame, don't immediately roll over and accept responsibility. Don't be too quick to kowtow to pressure or try to be peacekeeper. Stand firm when you're not in the wrong.

Be bold in all things, and in doing this affirm your strength. In this way you'll master *releasing an irresistible and overwhelming momentum.*

Sun Tzu on Emotional Maturity

Emotional maturity is a requirement for command for Sun Tzu. Right conduct is necessary for a general. He must be both enlightened and experienced in battle. Sun Tzu identifies five dangerous faults for a general and urges that these be meditated upon:

1. *If reckless, he can be killed;*
2. *If cowardly, captured;*
3. *If quick-tempered, he can be provoked to rage and make a fool of himself;*
4. *If he has too delicate a sense of honor, he is liable to fall into a trap because of an insult;*
5. *If he is of a compassionate nature, he may get bothered or upset.*

These are the five serious faults of a general, ruinous to the conduct of war. The ruin of the army and the death of the general are inevitable results of these five dangerous faults. They must be deeply pondered.

For Sun Tzu, unchecked ego has no place in leadership. As he says here, anger and resentment in decision-making are recipes for disaster: *A sovereign should not launch a war simply out of anger, not should a general fight a war simply out of resentment. Take action if it is to your advantage; cancel the action if it is not. An angered man can be happy again, just as a resentful one can feel pleased again, but a state that has perished can never revive, nor can a dead man be brought back to life. Therefore, with regards to the matter of war, the enlightened ruler is prudent, and the good general is full of caution.*

Great care for troops is always called for by Sun Tzu, but sentimentality for the people under his command is never to drive a general: *If, however, a general is indulgent towards his men but cannot employ them, cherishes them but cannot command them or inflict punishment on them when they violate the regulations, then they may be compared to spoiled children, and are useless for any practical purpose.*

Make Right Decisions

The general's power must always be in balance so the actions will be in order and the outcome virtuous: *If you are not sure of success, do not use troops. If you are not in danger, do not fight a battle.*

Decisions can't be made based on ego or on emotion. Just as Sun Tzu instructs his general, you must also keep your pride and sentimentality in check so you can allow your brain and your gut to respond appropriately. Otherwise, your decision-making will be driven by one of two extremes—personal pride or the fluid expectations of others. Both frequently have disastrous consequences.

Pride drives leaders and followers to take hasty, short-sighted actions that do damage both in the present and the future. If you let pride rule your decision-making, you'll burn influential bridges, develop a reputation as someone not to do business with or work for, and, as Sun Tzu cautions, fall into a trap made possible by a delicate sense of honor.

If you follow the whims of others and think too much about how your difficult decisions will impact them, you'll delay or avoid making the tough calls. You'll be exposed to worry and trouble. Many women in leadership have found that in times of turmoil, delaying the inevitable, such as layoffs and firings, ultimately does greater harm. As Sun Tzu advises, act quickly and decisively, and in the best interest of everyone who depends on you.

Power in the Wrong Place

The power of a sword wielded by an expert is incredible. To drive home a point, Nakamura Ryu Batto-Do instructor, Sensei David Drawdy, demonstrated how not to perform a downward cutting technique called *kirioroshi*. Rather than his typical smooth, effortless, crisp cuts, he clumsily allowed the blade to scoop and bounce at the end of the cut. The proper way is for the blade to float smoothly, then stop absolutely upon reaching its destination. It shouldn't recoil or jar. As he awkwardly wielded the blade, demonstrating incorrect use, he said, "That's wrong. That's too much power in the wrong places."

The problem, he explained, wasn't that the technique was too powerful or too strong. There's no such thing as a technique that's too powerful when it comes to implements designed to cut through metal body armor. The issue was that power was applied at the wrong times and in the wrong places.

You've almost certainly seen power applied in the wrong place many times in your career. It can be reckless spending by poor management, insecure managers who spend too much time covering up mistakes, or good people ill suited for their positions. These are all examples of misplaced power that leads to wasted energy and resources. Know yourself and strive to put your professional power where it belongs.

Apply Your Power Well

We all have a finite amount of energy to get us through the day. To always be at your best, use your resources wisely and apply them in the right ways, at the right time:

- If you're a gifted leader who spends half of your day doing administrative tasks better suited for an assistant, that's putting your energy in the wrong places.
- If you're a creative person who spends too much time in staff or client meetings when you should be generating new ideas or concepts, that's power in the wrong places.
- And if you're not in a position or a career that is suited to you, you're limiting your power altogether. You can't get that time back.

To gain mastery of your business, your career, and yourself, you must always work to put your finite power in the right places.

Are You Getting Better or Getting Beat Up?

Too much regard for the status quo is a pitfall for some women. Those who revere the status quo put loyalty ahead of their own business interests.

Of course, we all have to pay our dues during our careers. As with the rest of your life, you'll learn some of your best lessons in the most painful ways. This is how you get better. But there's such a thing as getting beaten up for no good reason, and it's happening in offices all over the world as you read this. Purpose-driven, goal-oriented improvement puts you ahead. Serving as the punching bag for someone else, even someone with good intentions, knocks you back.

Here's an example. When I was in college, I returned home regularly to train at a karate and kickboxing school. The owner of the school, Rob, had a younger brother who was preparing to test for his black belt. The younger brother, David, had a lot of heart and was driven to excel, both for himself and for his big brother's approval. Despite his drive, David's skill level never lived up to its potential. He lacked quality instruction and good mentoring to show him how to improve.

As he neared the time for his black belt test, I was encouraged because I knew that his big brother, who was an extremely skilled fighter, had agreed to work with him to get him ready. Finally, David was getting the one-on-one training he needed. From what I heard, Rob was really working him hard. I was excited to see the improvements he was making.

When I went back home and caught up with them, the reality fell short. True to form, David was working very hard. I had no doubt about that. But he wasn't getting any better. His skill level was stuck where it had been for quite a while. What had gone wrong? I found out when I talked to Rob. "I'm really working him," he boasted. "We put the gloves on everywhere—in the dojo, at his house, at my house, everywhere. I'm kicking his ass all the time."

I was starting to get the picture. Getting better is about much more than working harder. The gap in skill between the brothers was significant. Despite his best intentions, Rob didn't know how to effectively bring the younger brother up to his level. His idea of training him was to overtake him with his greater skills, batter and bruise him, and hope he would learn how not to get battered and bruised.

Some people can learn that way. Most can't. David, it was clear, couldn't. Rather than adapting teaching methods that weren't working, the older brother simply plowed through with what he knew, hopeful that it would take root.

The ending of the story of the brothers is telling. It wasn't long after these "ass-kicking" sessions that David tested for and received his black belt. Some months later he gave up martial arts. Despite his heart and willingness to be excellent, he never really improved. Not long after that, Rob quit too.

Staying the course, doing the same fruitless activities in the same way and expecting a different result, doesn't work. Taking beatings for their own sake is a formula for failure. You have to learn on your terms. And if you're a mentor or leader, be sure to direct others in ways that make a difference to them, not you.

Win Your Way

Alpha males are more likely than alpha females to see themselves as "exceptionally competent." This view of themselves contributes to their gravitation to high-risk and high-visibility competition. It's there that they can stand out and be seen. Alpha women, by comparison, are more inclined to shy away from competition, even when they have a good chance of winning.

Biology may have a lot to do with this. According to the National Institute of Mental Health, men are biologically more in need of adrenaline—and adrenaline comes with these high-pressure, high-risk situations. Women, however, thrive on the calming effect of endorphins that are produced in less look-at-me activities, like conversations and relationship building.

The authors of *Dancing on the Glass Ceiling*, Candy Deemer and Nancy Fredericks, put it this way: "We grew up in a world of intimacy and cooperation. Boys grow up in a world of status and competition." Despite this, competitiveness is certainly not only a masculine trait. Geraldine Laybourne believes women are highly competitive. We just define winning differently. For women to win, she says, "Everybody has to win. For my husband, he is not happy when we play Scrabble unless he wins. For me, I'm really happy if we both play well. I really am. I have to play well. I have to do well. But I don't actually have to see blood to be happy. And I think that's the biggest difference. It's not about somebody else losing."

To truly win, you must define victory for yourself, not by the standard of anyone else. To know what it means to win, you must know yourself.

BATTLEFIELD CHALLENGE

1. Have you ever changed the rules to manipulate circumstances in your favor in your career? How did this work out, and what did you learn from these experiences?
2. Name your five greatest strengths. Name your five greatest weaknesses. Challenge yourself by asking a trusted adviser to validate your personal assessment.
3. How have you put power in the wrong places? How can you better dedicate your time, resources, or attitude?

WOMAN WARRIOR

For Geraldine Laybourne, Trusting Your Instincts Means Knowing Yourself

Geraldine Laybourne knows the importance of leading with gut and instincts. She was chairman and CEO of Oxygen Media, as well as president of Disney/ABC Cable Networks.

She emphatically believes in the potential of instincts for women. "One of our best assets is our gut. Women often don't trust their instincts," she said. Laybourne has seen women devote themselves to working too hard on analysis instead. She sums it up this way: "Have good ideas, be creative—don't rationalize, just do."

A prerequisite to trusting your gut is being at peace with yourself. Laybourne always knew who she was, even as the only woman in the room early in her career. But she was confident in herself and trusted that she knew best. Today, she sees a declining trend in women pretending to be something they aren't to fit into a corporate culture defined by male traits. Women don't have to change who they are to belong. "They don't have to wear bow ties. And they don't have to talk in sports analogies," says Laybourne.

Chapter 14

Understanding and Leveraging Others

We don't accomplish anything in this world alone . . . and whatever happens is the result of the whole tapestry of one's life and all the weavings of individual threads from one to another that creates something.

—SANDRA DAY O'CONNOR

THE BATTLE: Your female attributes can be a powerful force in how you help, leverage, or overtake others. Resist the temptation to second-guess yours or you'll find yourself at a disadvantage in dealing with others.

THE CHAMPION: Use your heightened intuition, perception, and sensitivity toward the spoken and unspoken needs of others. This will enable you to collaborate with teams, communicate with clients and partners, and leverage deep understanding to overcome adversaries. Sun Tzu's methods of gaining insight about the enemy include gathering intelligence through spies and traitors. Today, most of us don't have a pool of professional saboteurs and spies. But you have other resources, not the least of which is within you. You must trust and refine your abilities to understand others—friends, enemies, and everyone in between.

t's just as important for you to understand your friends and enemies as it is for Sun Tzu. In the case of enemies, you must be able to read and assess them to anticipate and counter their attacks. This means honing your ability to stay one step ahead of them, see through their feints, and get to their real intentions. The same skills should also be leveraged for your interactions with clients, partners, and colleagues.

First, a word on enemies. You may not be reading this for literal and practical tips on how to launch a military campaign for the good of your state. "Enemy" may have a very broad application for you. This could be a hostile business partner or board member, a superior who's building a case against you, a colleague competing with you for a promotion, the Goliath in your industry, or any number of competing businesses.

No matter who your enemies are, it's critical that you understand them. If you're going to defeat them and expand your territory, you must also strike at the most opportune time with the right amount of well-placed force. If you know what motivates the enemy, you can exploit that, as Sun Tzu advises: *Offer a bait to allure the enemy, when he covets small advantages; strike the enemy when he is in disorder.*

Know Your Enemy

Sun Tzu doesn't talk much about intuition or using your gut, but he does call for constant vigilance and perception to discern the enemy's every move. It's critical to always be assessing him to know when he's strong and when he's weak: *Analyze the enemy's battle plan, so as to have a clear understanding of its strong and weak points. Agitate the enemy so as to ascertain his pattern of movement. Lure him in the open so as to find out his vulnerable spots in disposition. Probe him and learn where his strength is abundant and where deficient.*

Don't expect your enemy to reveal her weaknesses. You must help her to do so. How well you know the enemy and apply that knowledge will be a deciding factor in determining victory. According to Sun Tzu: *It is necessary for a wise general to make correct assessments of the enemy's situation to create conditions leading to victory and to calculate distances and the degree of difficulty of the terrain. He who knows these things and applies them to fighting will definitely win.*

Nina DiSesa, the chairman and chief creative officer of McCann New York, says she's seen women climb the rungs of success, then let their guard down. She observes that while women may have risen because of their intuition and skills in reading and understanding people, they set those abilities aside once they achieve success. Instead, those under the newly promoted manager are now focused on sucking up to her. DiSesa observes these women shift from reading others to being read, and they forget they're not invincible.

Time Your Attacks

As Sun Tzu says repeatedly, timing is a major part of understanding enemies. You must know when to strike and when to wait for a better opportunity: *He refrains from intercepting an enemy whose banners are in perfect order, and desists from attacking an army whose formations are in an impressive array. This is the art of assessing circumstances.*

Know what you're up against, assess the conditions, and launch your attack when the time is right.

Sun Tzu offers more insight into when the time is and isn't right to launch an assault. Whether you're moving a corporation, a division, a team, or yourself, follow these guidelines: *The art of employing troops is that when the enemy occupies high ground, do not confront him uphill, and when his back is resting on hills, do not make a frontal attack. When he pretends to flee, do not pursue. Do not attack soldiers whose temper is keen. Do not swallow a bait offered by the enemy. Do not thwart an enemy who is returning homewards.*

When your adversary is in a position of strength, don't attack. When he's backed by hills you can't see beyond, don't attack him head-on where he can see you advance. Read him well so you can tell when he's feinting in an attempt to lure you into a trap. Don't attack when his temper is at its sharpest. Don't attack an enemy who's in a position that he'll do anything to defend.

Instead, attack when he's vulnerable. Exploit his weaknesses. Sun Tzu is writing here of the general who has done well to evaluate his enemy's weaknesses: *His offensive will be irresistible if he plunges into the enemy's weak points; he cannot be overtaken when he withdraws if he moves swiftly. Hence, if we wish to fight, the enemy will be compelled to an engagement even though he is safe behind high ramparts and deep ditches. This is because we attack a position he must relieve.*

Read the Signs

Sun Tzu urges repeatedly to stay attentive to the signs of your enemy's condition: *If the banners are shifting about, sedition is afoot. If the officers are angry, it means that men are weary. When the enemy feeds his horses with grain, kills the beasts of burden for food and packs up the utensils used for drawing water, he shows no intention to return to his tents and is determined to fight to the death.*

You'll make informed decisions and execute well by gathering this kind of telltale information. Establish the signs for knowing when your competitor is weak and when strong so you'll be able to time and launch your attacks for speedy and decisive wins.

Plan Your Attack

Knowledge and data points are critical. So, too, is flawless execution. Not all conditions are beneficial for launching an attack. Sun Tzu says to avoid your enemy's positions of strengths. Instead, assault his strategy: *The best policy in war is to attack the enemy's strategy. The second best way is to disrupt his alliances through diplomatic means. The next best method is to attack his army in the field. The worst policy is to attack walled cities. Attacking cities is the last resort when there is no alternative.*

Attacking your adversary's strategy is a profound concept and far more complex than launching a full-on attack. The worst approach is to attack an entrenched enemy who is well defended. This is difficult and costly in resources and people. You would do well to study this passage and define what it means for you to *attack the enemy's strategy*.

The Orchestra Conductor

Your skills in understanding others apply to much more than your enemies. They also relate to teammates, partners, and others. Heffernan concludes that women's leadership styles are frequently about unleashing the potential of others. In her book *How She Does It*, Heffernan likens it to the conductor of an orchestra. These women bring out the best of each player and foster results that are greater than the sum of all individual parts.

Unleashing the potential of others is critical to Sun Tzu, who again says this about the importance of choosing and using good troops: *A skilled commander sets great store by using the situation to the best advantage, and does not make excessive demands on his subordinates. Hence he is able to select the right men and exploits the situation. He who takes advantage of the situation uses his men in fighting as rolling logs or rocks. It is the nature of logs and rocks to stay stationary on the flat ground, and to roll forward on a slope. If four-cornered, they stop; if round-shaped, they roll. Thus, the energy of troops skillfully commanded is just like the momentum of round rocks quickly tumbling down from a mountain thousands of feet in height. That is what "use of energy" means.*

Sun Tzu's concept is similar to Heffernan's. The skilled leader builds strong teams that work together to create magnificent results. He knows how to direct teams and when to get out of their way so they can perform mightily.

Geraldine Laybourne has put this idea into practice throughout her career. Her management philosophy was formed early as a teacher in an open-education, individualized-instruction environment. When she became a manager, she called on this methodology of discerning the attributes of each individual. She says it was a gratifying process to find out how great her team was and to leverage the best of each person.

The Way to Consensus

Many women lead based on a consensus-building model. This isn't to say they aren't capable of making tough decisions on their own. They simply value the collaborative nature of their teams. To build consensus, you have to be willing and able to listen and look for ways to help other succeed. For good managers, this means fostering an environment that gives everyone a voice. Throughout her career, Laybourne has seen a dynamic that may be familiar to you. A woman will make a contribution in a meeting and it goes unacknowledged. But then, ten minutes later, a man says the same thing and it's acknowledged and possibly even applauded.

"But we never let that happen," says Laybourne of her time in leadership. "If Sara Levinson said something, I would repeat it if I felt she wasn't heard. And then when somebody would take credit for her idea ten minutes later, I said, 'Good for you, supporting Sara!'" she recalls.

Collaboration over Domination

In *Alpha Male Syndrome,* Kate Ludeman and Eddie Erlandson pull from their coaching experience and a growing body of scientific research. They conclude, naturally, that female alphas are ambitious and drawn to positions of authority. But alpha women are much less inclined to a domination-oriented leadership style. They're better attuned to the emotional climate they operate in, and more likely than alpha males to look for ways to collaborate and look for win-wins. These women tend to look for consensus instead of simply imposing their will. The authors sum it up this way: "In other words, alpha women want to lead, but they don't necessarily need to rule."

Ludeman and Erlandson make an interesting contrast between alpha males and alpha females when it comes to professional relationships: "Men tend to look at their business relationships in a hierarchical or competitive context, as opportunities to establish power and dominance. This makes it possible to have functional relationships but not *rich* relationships, because a certain level of trust can never be part of the exchange. Women, however, approach their business relationships in a cooperative context, as opportunities to establish connections," they conclude.

Alpha female and former eBay CEO Meg Whitman serves as a good example of the contrasts in leadership styles of alpha males and females. Whitman, like most alphas of both genders, enjoys being in command. She's driven by metrics, and known for the results she's created in her career. She's been named *Fortune* magazine's most powerful woman in American business. She's also known for her advanced empathizing skills, active and fair listening skills, and collaborative style.

Empower Teams

It's these collaboration skills that have led Whitman to build exceptional teams, like those at eBay. The Internet company grew sevenfold during her leadership. Tom Tierney, an eBay board member, says, "Her most striking attribute is to enable other people and other groups to get things done." While the tough-minded, competitive nature Whitman has is common among alpha males, traits like collaboration and empathizing aren't identified among the vast majority of alpha males Ludeman and Erlandson studied.

Sun Tzu recognizes that empowering troops entails meeting their needs so they can do their best always: *Pay attention to the soldiers' well-being and do not fatigue them. Try to keep them in high spirits and conserve their energy.*

Teams are most effective when people are utilized to their maximum potential, led well, and have their needs met. This takes understanding of the people who are fighting for you. To follow Sun Tzu's direction, be attentive to your team, ensure that the right people are in the right positions, and be sure leadership demonstrates their high regard for talent. Demonstrate your care for your people and they'll demonstrate their loyalty when it matters most.

Sun Tzu on Alliances

No business or battlefield discussion of understanding others is complete without a discussion of your allies. Sun Tzu's insights are timeless. First, he instructs, you must know what you're getting into when forming alliances: *One who is not acquainted with the designs of his neighbors should not enter into alliances with them.*

A simple idea, but how many times have you seen this wisdom discounted by over-eager business partners who rush too quickly into an agreement? Just as you would thoroughly assess an enemy, you should completely evaluate a potential ally before forming a significant bond. The deeper and more valued the alliance, the better you must know the other party.

The right alliances will be of great benefit: *Those who do not know the conditions of mountains and forests, hazardous defiles, marshes and swamps, cannot conduct the march of an army. Those who do not use local guides are unable to obtain the advantage of the ground.*

You can't succeed without knowing the details and landscapes of hostile territories. Powerful partnerships can go a long way in helping you gain an effective picture of a new opportunity. Importantly, Sun Tzu cautions to be sure to consider the other party's motivation. Many corporate partnership agreements aren't worth the paper they're printed on because there's no tangible long-term strategy for maximizing the initial efforts, or clear benefit for both parties.

Understand what the other party wants the alliance to accomplish. In reality, will it ever go anywhere? Is the other party vested? If not, you're better off using your efforts for more worthwhile activities that will build your business.

Many small and midsized businesses that attempt to build partnerships with large organizations don't discern what's in it for the big firm. These agreements either go nowhere or end up being more trouble than they're worth because the larger company has no incentive to act. Build alliances that will benefit you both. Otherwise, you may discover—after expending lots of time, tedious effort, and money—that the big guys don't need you nearly as much as you need them. Of a mighty army, Sun Tzu says: *One does not need to seek alliances with other neighboring states, nor is there any need to foster the power of other states, but only to pursue one's own strategic designs to overawe his enemy.*

BATTLEFIELD CHALLENGE

1. Do you find yourself stifling your intuitive nature to focus more on logic and data when it comes to understanding others? If so, how could shifting that balance help you be more effective?

2. Are you a consensus builder? If so, are you in an environment where these skills are valued? If not, what can you do to influence the culture to develop one of consensus building?

3. Attacking your adversary's strategy is a profound concept. Think about a time when you've done this or seen it done. How can you utilize this to overtake your competitors today?

Understanding Others Makes Business Sense for Marion Luna Brem

Marion Luna Brem was married with two young boys when her happy home life was ripped apart with her diagnosis of a terminal illness. She was 30 years old and given two to five years to live. Within weeks of each other, she had a hysterectomy and a mastectomy. All of her hair fell out from chemotherapy.

She was fighting cancer without health insurance, unemployed, newly divorced—and the head of her household. With no resume, she followed the counsel of her best friend who encouraged her to try sales. Sixteen interviews later, she got a job in one of the most cliché male environments—car sales. It was a good move. By the end of her first year, she was salesperson of the year. At 36, she opened her dealership, Love Chrysler, which has become a multimillion-dollar enterprise.

In Brem's experience, she's noted that women are good at reading and determining others' hot buttons. Brem believes women speak directly to a person's "life purpose, their source of personal energy, the things that give meaning and drive to their life..." She says this gives women an advantage in connecting and selling. Women listen to what's said, and, importantly, what's not said.

Brem's sales philosophy has been simple, but not obvious. She calls it "engaging with heart." For a woman going through a divorce, she sent a "hang in there" card. When a customer decided to put a family member into a nursing home, Brem sent flowers and an encouraging note. On the last day of schools, customers who were teachers received a "you did it!" card.

She believes her gender has been an advantage in an industry full of men. It's enabled her to use her intuition and be attentive to buyers' needs. She also believes in staying in touch with her emotions. Because of this transparency, buyers are comfortable being candid with her.

These strategies of understanding others have been a major asset to Brem. She's an *Inc.* magazine Entrepreneur of the Year, ranked in both *Hispanic Business* and *Working Woman* magazines Top 100, and is a member of The International Automotive Hall of Fame.

Chapter 15

Practice the Basics

孫子

Life's too short. Get over it. Move on to the next thing.

—CONDOLEEZZA RICE

> **THE BATTLE:** Distractions masquerading as opportunities, impatience, and lack of focus can daily distract you from strategic objectives. So, too, can trying to please others and playing too much by the rules. These diversions can cause you to lose track of the fundamentals of advancing your career and driving your business.
>
> **THE CHAMPION:** To achieve bold success, you'll need to continuously put into practice deep understanding of the fundamentals. Be focused, consistent, and principled, and demonstrate what's important in your every action.

Whether we're talking about sales, leadership, warfare, parenting, or sports, the basics are simple, reliable truths. It's in the basics where wisdom is cultivated. Basics are just as essential in your profession as they are for Sun Tzu. You must study circumstances deeply and dedicate time to maintaining your edge.

Elegant in its simplicity, *The Art of War* focuses on fundamentals. This simple, proven brilliance is why Sun Tzu is studied with such intensity today. In the 2,500 years since he wrote this work, the world has changed. Weaponry has repeatedly been revolutionized. The scale of battle has increased thousandsfold. But Sun Tzu's basic truths haven't changed.

In Sun Tzu's day, innovation looked very different. His natural state was combat and his vehicle was war. But innovation had the same purpose then as it does for us now—bettering the lives and fortunes of our people. It's always all about the basics.

Meditations on Fundamental Principles

To be victorious, Sun Tzu urges that you always obey these five fundamental principles:

1. *He who knows when to fight and when not to fight will win.*
2. *He who understands how to handle both superior and inferior forces will win.*
3. *He whose ranks are united in purpose will win.*
4. *He who is well prepared and lies in wait for an enemy who is not well prepared will win.*
5. *He whose generals are able and not interfered with by the sovereign will win.*

It is in these five points that the way to victory is known.

There is a great deal to consider in these five principles. You can read them quickly, but I recommend you study them deeply.

The first principle is to only fight when it's to your advantage. If you can't win, find another option besides battle. Evade, retreat, or outwit your way out of the conflict. Battles are costly and wasteful. If battle is the only option, fight another day when the odds are in your favor.

If you do fight, you must know you are able to win the battle before you initiate it. Moreover, each battle you fight must be to your benefit, whether you're fighting for yourself, your business, or a team: *If not in the interest of the state, do not act. If you are not sure of success, do not use troops. If you are not in danger, do not fight a battle. . . . Therefore, with regard to the matter of war, the enlightened ruler is prudent, and the good general is full of caution. Thus, the state is kept secure and the army preserved.*

These basic principles are the essence of Sun Tzu's battlefield strategy.

Know the Enemy's Plan

For Sun Tzu, knowing the enemy is among the most elementary aspects of battle. If you don't know them, you won't be able to match them on the battlefield, in the sales showdown, or on any competitive playing field. This is Sun Tzu's call for keeping your Strengths, Weaknesses, Opportunities, and Threats (SWOT) analysis current and acting on it: *Analyze the enemy's battle plan, so as to have a clear understanding of its strong and weak points.*

To know the enemy, he directs readers on, among other things, the use of spies: *Now, the reason that the enlightened sovereign and the wise general conquer the enemy whenever they move and their achievements surpass those of ordinary men is that they have foreknowledge. . . . It must be obtained by ordinary men who know the enemy situation.*

You probably don't have a cadre of spies doing your business's bidding. But you certainly do have access to resources that can help you create a full picture of your market, provide competitive intelligence on leaders and emerging firms, and keep you informed of evolving knowledge of key players, trends, and technologies. So much information is in the public domain today that keeping tabs on your competitors' public data is easy. Subscription services and research firms abound. Utilize tools that are within your means. Also use your networks to stay ahead of your adversaries, keeping them on the move so you may always have the upper hand. Use every valid tool at your disposal.

Seeking the Blossoms, Miss the Fruit

No matter how much money you make, how successful you are, or how many advanced degrees you have, the basics must always be at the forefront for you. You must always practice and study them. Just because they're simple doesn't mean they're easy or well comprehended by others.

As mentioned earlier, Miyamoto Musashi was the greatest swordsman who ever lived. He warned almost 400 years ago in the Japanese classic, *The Book of Five Rings*, that we shouldn't be so concerned with the blossoms of a tree that we ignore the fruit. Musashi isn't saying we should ignore the flowers. Not at all. In addition to being a brilliant warrior, he was a painter, poet, and gardener. He appreciated beauty. But he knew to remember the substance of what matters. Always keep your business objective in focus.

The tendency to be sidelined by distractions and window-dressing is seen again and again in organizations of all sizes. It's tempting to lose sight of objectives in satisfying the need of the minute. We often give disproportionate attention to less meaningful and less critical factors that conflict with our overall goals. Other times, the excitement generated by a new idea, trend, or concept is contagious before its value is proven.

This misplaced focus leads to the ironies and disconnects that abound between a company's mission and its day-to-day practices. You see this all the time: Telecommunications companies with internal voice-mail systems that don't work. Web design firms with horrible websites. Customer service departments in which you can rarely reach a representative to help, and when you do, the call gets dropped. Professional printers with business cards that look like they were printed at the local quick-print shop. When organizations take their focus off of who they are and what they do, the basics are elusive. They get caught up in the fleeting blossoms.

The Path to Failure

The event discussed in this section takes place in a jujitsu dojo, but similar scenarios happen every day in businesses around the world. This was a student, but it could just as easily apply to the chairman of your board.

An impatient student believes his level of skill is great. He approaches his teacher and tells her he's ready to be promoted to the next level of black belt. The student's not ready, of course. If he had been, the instructor would have already told him he was.

The seasoned instructor agrees that a test is in order. She calls her most senior students and shares with them the parameters of the test. This would be a test designed to introduce humility to the candidate. To pass, he'd have to perform extraordinarily.

On test day, the student arrives, ready to show his stuff. The instructor and senior students are ready to demonstrate to him how much he doesn't yet know. As expected, it doesn't go well for the candidate. He fails the test publicly. The failure badly damages his robust ego. But that's not the worst of it. People fail tests all the time. The real shame is that the student is embarrassed because he's unable to demonstrate basic concepts and techniques. His arrogance had taken over and he'd convinced himself that he was so skillful that he no longer needed to practice fundamentals. They were beneath him. The reality, however, was clear to everyone but him. Rather than being full of skill, he was full of something else.

This brash student was caught up with fancy, flashy techniques. He had lost touch with the fundamentals, and so he lost touch with everything.

Unlike women who are true experts and who boldly step up to ask for what they want, the student was ill-equipped to achieve the results he sought. If he had deeply understood the basics and challenged himself to apply them in more and greater ways, he'd have achieved what he wanted without having to ask for it.

When Business Basics Atrophy

It's no coincidence that arrogance and impatience are accompanied by an atrophying of the basics. We've all had experiences like this one: I tried repeatedly to reach a sales representative to place a bulk order for books by a sales guru. This expert espoused the virtues of having a sales engine in place to provide impeccable customer service. The problem was, said guru *didn't* have a sales engine in place—or much in the way of customer service, either. When someone did respond to me weeks later, it was too little, too late. The company had lost track of basic business fundamentals, as well as its mission. To me, their credibility was shot.

You see failure to accomplish the basics all the time. Salespeople who have forgotten the fundamentals of connecting on a personal level can no longer close the deals they used to. Account representatives neglect the basics of managing clients, like returning phone calls and following through with delivery timelines. They lose valuable accounts in the process. Leaders who set terrible examples but expect their people to be above reproach soon won't have followers of any caliber.

Get Past Complexity to Understand Simplicity

In addition to simply forgetting about the basics, many companies make the mistake of letting unnecessary complexity get in the way of the basics—the basics being the achievement of the company's goals.

A good example is a company I was working with to launch its website. The business objective was clear: launch the website by a set date so the company could bring a promising new product to market. Other deliverables were contingent upon this launch. Unfortunately, led by the indecisiveness of the CEO and the rest of the very flat management team, the company couldn't divorce itself from issues like the precise color of the background frames and other tiny nuances. They waffled back and forth, fiddling with little things. Everyone had their own ideas.

These issues were insignificant and irrelevant to the goal of the site. The company wouldn't sell one dollar more or less of product based on these technicalities. But the launch of the site and product was delayed substantially as they wrestled with them. Ultimately, this cost them money and time. They got caught up in the flowers and lost sight of the business objective.

Experts at multitasking, it's common for mid-level and even senior-level women to be highly skilled tacticians. These women are great with details, expert at tracking even complex components. These important skills and this level of detail are essential in all businesses. But the danger is in getting so mired in the day-to-day details that the big picture is compromised. No matter how deep you are in studying a problem and developing a solution, always keep the bottom line top of mind.

A Punch Is Just a Punch

Martial arts philosopher Bruce Lee illuminates what it means to get past complexity to understand simplicity. Lee had an epiphany many years into his martial arts training that's replete with life lessons. "Before I studied the art, a punch to me was just a punch, a kick was just a kick. After I'd studied the art, a punch was no longer a punch, a kick no longer a kick. Now that I understand the art, a punch is just a punch, a kick is just a kick."

This is the state of so fully understanding something that its simplicity is finally revealed, as in "Grasp the Essence" in Chapter 12:

"Preparedness." This only happens at mastery. Until then, it's a lot of blossoms and a little fruit.

The Soul of Simplicity in Action

In a commencement address she delivered shortly after leaving HP, Carly Fiorina expressed what it means to get to the heart of simplicity. "Most people will judge you by what they see on the outside," she said. "Only you and God will know what's on the inside. But at the end of your life, if people ask you what your greatest accomplishment was, my guess is, it will be something that happened inside you, that no one else ever saw, something that had nothing to do with outside success, and everything to do with how you decide to live in the world."

Wanting Isn't Enough—Discipline Is Mandatory

Starting and growing a business requires extraordinary responsibility and commitment. The fate of families, employees, investors, partners, and even communities may hang in the balance. Most entrepreneurs begin their businesses with a big dream and a little capital. They're passionate about their business and what they offer the market. More than anything, they want to make their dreams come true. They'll do whatever it takes.

To this end, they often work very hard and sometimes very smart. Their vision is to create a better company, product, or service delivery mechanism. But sometimes that passion is extinguished before it can blaze. Burnout, unexpected obstacles, unrealistic revenue projections, down economies, poor management, and flawed business models all can contribute to this. That which they wanted more than anything has lost its urgency. The shiny new toy isn't so shiny or so new. All that's left is hard work, long hours, and uncertainty.

Entrepreneurs know the data. Only about half of all small businesses will survive their first five years. Starting a business isn't that difficult. But growing a business—that's the real challenge.

Having Is the Hard Part

Marsha Serlin knows what it means to be a small business owner during difficult times. She also knows what it means to persevere and apply discipline to achieve success. "There's nothing more satisfying than when you do it for yourself, against all odds," she says. "When the light is the most dim, it's probably when there's the most promise. And don't quit too fast! My sage advice: Get your business to the third year, and then you can sail. We all want instant success, but you have to build the foundation of any business."

A now-defunct karate school is a perfect example of how hard it is to keep a small business going once the excitement is gone. The assistant instructor, Mark, wanted few things more than to run his own school. He tirelessly put together business plans and curricula. He researched places to rent and talked with potential landlords and business partners. Then one day, after a few years of dreaming and planning, the head instructor of Mark's school quietly announced he was stepping down. He had lost his desire to train and to teach. He told Mark, "You finally got what you wanted. The school is yours." He turned over the keys and walked away.

Mark was given a tremendous gift. He had an active, dues-paying student body who knew him, respected him, and was enthusiastic about learning from him. He was given a school with a good reputation that had been around for a decade. He was given a wonderful relationship with a landlord who required only very reasonable rent. The equipment, including mats, mirrors, weapons, and sparring gear, would have cost thousands to purchase new and would have been nearly impossible to find used in pre-eBay days. His dream had come true—and then some!

But just brief months later, Mark had lost his dedication. He missed class frequently to spend time with a new girlfriend and pursue other miscellaneous adventures. He was soon asked to step down by students, their parents, and the landlord. Mark's second in command, Stephanie, took over. She, too, was brimming with enthusiasm, but she didn't have the leadership qualities to keep things going. She soon lost heart and the school closed for good.

For Mark and Stephanie, wanting was easy. Having and keeping were the hard parts.

Discipline and the Basics

Anybody can want. The lucky can receive. It takes discipline and consistency to receive, keep, and grow. This is true whether you're managing thousands, a small team, or your own career path. Discipline is fundamental.

Sun Tzu writes about the impact of consistency on implementation: *If orders are consistently carried out and the troops are strictly supervised, they will be obedient. If orders are never carried out, they will be disobedient. And the smooth implementation of orders reflects harmonious relationship between the commander and his troops.*

A Special Invitation

Nancy, an internationally renowned martial arts instructor, was invited to participate in a very special advanced class. This was a session with world-renown Japanese karate practitioners who were visiting the United States. Nancy was excited about what they'd practice and the amount of knowledge she'd gather in that session. She let herself fantasize: "What will they work on? Will they explain deep meaning behind some of the more traditional techniques I've always wondered about? I'll probably see techniques I've never seen before!"

The special advanced class was held in a private, closed-door area. This was only for the privileged few who had been invited to attend and who were deemed ready to learn the advanced material. There she was, one of a handful of very senior, very experienced martial artists who had been training seriously for decades.

But what she experienced surprised her: "We trained for two hours and drilled one kick, the front kick, the entire time." The instructor's goal was to get each student to measurably increase power with that kick. To do that, he showed them how to improve the hip angle and hip torque in ways Nancy had never practiced before. "I always knew that piece was in there, but had never really understood it until we delved deeply into it in that class," she says.

For Nancy and for everyone else, that intensive, closed-door session was a lesson in both the fundamentals and the more subtle nuances that comprise the basics. To understand the nuances and to leverage that understanding, they had to first deeply understand the basics. "I won't say something was great just because it was in private and taught by the top instructors in the system. But that class dramatically improved the way I perform that simple kick. It gave me new insight into something I thought I understood extremely well," she said.

In the same way, through earnest discipline and with the humility to practice the basics, you can learn and understand the elegant simplicity of your profession.

No Easy Way

If you're going to be successful in business, you've got to be committed to some very serious training. To lead and inspire others, you must be inspired yourself. You can't motivate staff, partners, or clients if you're coasting. And you can't live off of dreams. They're only for the beginning. Once you accomplish what you set out to do, set bigger goals. Revisit your plans regularly to stay on track. Ask yourself if you're making the most of the goals you've achieved.

Mastery only comes with discipline, sacrifice, and an always-renewed focus on the basics. There are no shortcuts to this kind of understanding.

Poor Conditioning

The basics are simple. But that doesn't mean they're commonly practiced, or even well understood by many people. Those who truly understand the fundamentals know how to adapt them to real scenarios. Sun Tzu tells us here again that this is beyond the comprehension of many: *Even though we show people the victory gained by using flexible tactics in conformity to the changing situations, they do not comprehend this. People all know the tactics by which we achieved victory, but they do not know how the tactics were applied in the situation to defeat the enemy.*

Understanding and practicing the basics requires self-evaluation. Just because you were taught something one way doesn't mean you were taught it properly. And even if it was right at the time, circumstances change. It's easy to pick up bad habits.

The reason athletes train with such great repetition is because of the importance of muscle memory. Muscle memory is the repetition of a motor movement with such consistency that a memory is created for the muscle. Ultimately, the motion will be performed without deliberate thought. It just happens. You've experienced this in any sports you've played, in riding a bicycle, and in typing. This can be applied to any of the basics in your career. If you practice them over and over, you'll perform them without intentional thought. They become part of you.

The down side to this phenomenon is that not all conditioning is positive. The bad habits and poor conditioning you acquire along the way will harm your professional performance.

Bad habits compromise your success. Maybe it's starting the workday by "quickly" checking personal e-mails. The next thing you know, you've blown thirty minutes. Or maybe it's taking leisurely lunches. A few minutes here and there won't hurt, right? They hurt when they become habits. Providing sloppy, unedited presentations and reports as a matter of course will ultimately become your standard.

I'm sure you can list plenty of other examples of how poor conditioning can truncate your potential in little ways that will ultimately become big obstacles.

Make understanding and practicing sound basics and eliminating poor conditioning habits you take up daily.

BATTLEFIELD CHALLENGE

1. How often do you go back and re-evaluate your performance against the basic tenets that will lead you to success? Build in regular reviews for this.

2. Think about a time when fundamentals eluded you, when you got caught up in a personality struggle, paid too much attention to inconsequential details, or otherwise lost focus on the business objective. What do you think caused you to get off course?

3. Review the section titled "Meditations on Fundamental Principles." What are the five to ten most critical basics of your business? How have you increased your understanding of them over the past year? About which basic do you have the most to learn?

The Basics Didn't Come Easily for Wilma Rudolph

Wilma Rudolph was crippled by polio at a young age and told she'd never walk again. Less than a decade later, in the 1960 Olympics, she became the first American woman to win three gold medals.

Rudolph was born prematurely in segregated Clarksville, Tennessee, weighing only four and a half pounds. She was born into a big family led by hard-working black parents. Her father was a railroad porter and handyman and her mother worked as a housekeeper for wealthy white families. Her parents were rich in love but poor by most other standards.

Rudolph was frequently ill as a child. The family didn't have access to quality medical care, so Rudolph's mother tended to her daughter's many illnesses—measles, mumps, scarlet fever, chickenpox, double pneumonia. But the worst was polio, which left her crippled.

Fortunately, her mother wouldn't accept defeat. Unable to receive treatment closer to home, she took Rudolph to a black medical college in Nashville. They made the fifty-mile trip for treatment and therapy twice a week for two years until finally Rudolph was able to walk with a metal leg brace. By the time she was twelve, she could walk without the brace. Performing the basics required an enormous investment of time, energy, and effort. She wasn't content simply to walk. She wanted to run. More than that, she wanted to be an athlete.

In junior high, Rudolph joined the basketball team, but it was three years before she was put into a game. In her sophomore year, she was spotted by Ed Temple, the coach for the Tennessee State University women's track team. He invited her to Tennessee State for a summer sports camp. Later, she received a full scholarship to that university.

Rudolph set state records in basketball and led her team to a state championship, but she's best known as a runner. She competed in her first Olympic Games in 1956 at sixteen and took a bronze medal in the 4 x 4 relay. In 1960, in Rome, she won the 100-meter dash, the 200-meter dash, and ran the anchor on the 400-meter relay team. This led her to great fame and broke gender barriers in track-and-field events.

Rudolph was a trailblazer with an illustrious career. But there was one first that shows how she practiced the basics in her life. Upon her triumphant return home, the Olympian insisted that the homecoming parade and banquet the town held in her honor be unsegregated. She went on to participate in protests until segregation laws were struck down in the city.

Chapter 16

Battlefield Wisdom

Every great dream begins with a dreamer. Always remember,
you have within you the strength, the patience, and the passion to
reach for the stars to change the world.
—HARRIET TUBMAN

> THE BATTLE: You struggle daily to meet deadlines and keep
> all the balls you're juggling from crashing to the floor. But
> success is about much more than accomplishing tasks, even
> important ones. It requires consistently exercising wisdom.
>
> THE CHAMPION: The exceptional execute based on the wisdom
> that can only be amassed from years in figurative trenches and
> on battlefields.

The Art of War is a treatise of battlefield wisdom. Much of the book
could certainly apply to this chapter, but here we'll focus on some
un-common-sense strategies you can apply to achieve uncommon
success.

Less Is More: Pick Your Battles

Every now and then, you've probably found yourself engaging in a conflict out of a visceral reaction, rather than an intentional plan of action. Maybe your competence is called into question, you're publicly belittled, your pride is hurt, or you get caught up in the heat of the moment. There will be many battles you will be tempted to fight, but should avoid. Some should never be fought. Others should be handled on a different day under conditions more beneficial to you. A recurrent theme that serves as a concise summary of *The Art of War* is this: *He who knows when to fight and when not to fight will win.*

Fight on Your Terms

Former Lucent CEO Pat Russo's account is briefly mentioned earlier. She went through many battles at the helm of the *Fortune* 500 telecom company. But earlier in her career she had learned when it was worthwhile to fight and when it wasn't. When she was on boards and in other senior positions, she was frequently mistaken for the secretary and asked to fetch coffee. As a marketing rep for IBM, she was assigned an account with an organization that refused to work with her because she was a woman. Her reaction was to move on to battles that were worth fighting and focus her best performance there.

Depending on what's at stake, there are battles you'll need to fight instead of walking away. Early in Carly Fiorina's career, she was an entry-level salesperson at AT&T. The first time her boss introduced her to a client, he said, "This is Carly Fiorina, our token bimbo." She laughed to mask her embarrassment, but after the meeting, Fiorina went to her boss and said, "You will never do that to me again." Narrow-minded clients and short-sighted board members are one thing. A boss you have to work with day in and day out is another matter.

It's not always easy to know when to stand your ground and fight for your principles and yourself, and when to avoid or postpone the conflict. But for Sun Tzu, the decision is simple. You do battle when, and only when, you have enough to gain by fighting to make it worthwhile. As Sun Tzu says in Lionel Giles's translation: *Take action if it is to your advantage; cancel the action if it is not.*

About changing your position relative to the battlefield, Sun Tzu puts it clearly: *Move only if there is a real advantage to be gained.*

He also offers caution in attacking a stronger army. If it's in your best interest to battle a mightier opponent, be sure to execute when the enemy is most susceptible to defeat. Avoid attacking a strong army: *A clever commander, therefore, avoids the enemy when his spirit is keen and attacks him when it is lost. This is the art of attaching importance to moods.*

Leave the Ego for the Enemy

Because humility is the heart of wisdom, pride is never on Sun Tzu's list of territories to be defended. Engaging in battle carries with it mammoth responsibility, both for you and the people on your team: *The general who understands war is the controller of his people's fate and the guarantor of the security of the nation.*

Those are some audacious obligations. Even if you're not in the business of securing the sovereignty of a nation, you most certainly have a role in the fates of your business and your customers. To be excellent, fight the hard battles when you have something to gain and always work toward possessing the maturity and perspective to understand when you don't.

Different Enemies, Different Strategies

Each enemy is different, and you must know him to be able to defeat him. This is another recurrent theme of *The Art of War*: *Know the enemy and know yourself, and you can fight a hundred battles with no danger of defeat.*

There's no substitute for this enlightened knowledge and for fore-knowledge gained from intelligence sources. The general who doesn't understand the enemy will lose. For Sun Tzu, that's justice. It's battlefield karma. To win, you must fully understand your adversary. His strength and spirit should be measured and you should take action accordingly: *If he is well prepared with substantial strength, take double precautions against him. If he is powerful in action, evade him. If he is angry, seek to discourage him. If he appears humble, make him arrogant. If his forces have taken a good rest, wear them down. If his forces are united, divide them. . . . Launch the attack where he is unprepared; take action when it is unexpected. . . . These are the keys to victory for a strategist.*

The idea of exploiting the enemy's ego—and the importance of keeping yours out of the equation—is repeated in that passage.

Everything Is Critical

During one of my first sword classes, a senior named Ken was assigned to help me better grasp the most basic movements. Before I had so much as drawn my sword, he said something that has always stayed with me: "When working with the sword, everything is critical."

Momentary inattentiveness and even "little" mistakes when using a live, sharp sword can cause very serious injury. But "everything is critical" means more than just how to avoid getting cut.

Learning to use a sword is a precision experience. Tiny angles, the slightest alteration of hand position, shades of foot positioning, and other very small elements that are imperceptible to the untrained eye are important. The slightest bend in the knees, sinking of the hips, and position of the hands translate to very large differences in the successful direction and power of each cut. If these "little things" aren't studied seriously and internalized by the student, the big things will never work. Proper technique and application require great attention to the little things. The minute details are essential elements of the big picture. Everything truly is critical.

Mind the Details in Business

In business, if you ignore the little things, you miss a lot. You must be attentive to the slightest cues from prospects that will help you understand how to make a sale. You must listen to what a client is and isn't saying to circumvent potential problems. What's his real concern with the scope of work? What isn't he saying that will make the difference between buying from you or from your competitor? If your standard is excellence, everything is critical—from unintended body language to tiny cues unintentionally dropped.

If you're operating in a less than exceptional way, you gloss over what you perceive to be the little things. You opt out of the training your company offers. You downplay the importance of keeping track of industry trends. You decide not to spend the extra time doing the research for the big sales pitch. You don't bother to read the latest industry research report.

The result? You're passed over for promotion. Your competitor, knowing everything is critical, delivers a spot-on presentation that wins the business. Your business partner chooses to team with another company for the massive proposal.

If you're a leader who doesn't understand that everything is critical, you may assume that your best people are content with their challenges and compensation structure. So you don't take any initiative, no matter how small, to make sure they're happy. Good people will eventually move on to organizations whose leadership demonstrates how much everything matters in how they regard their teams. All that will be left to you are the mediocre staff. They don't tend to the little things either.

When you recognize that it's all critical, you employ precision focus and require the highest standards of yourself and everyone around you.

You also reduce the number of mistakes and miscalculations you make. To quote this challenging passage from Sun Tzu once more: *He wins his victories without making mistakes. Making no mistakes is what establishes the certainty of victory, for it means that he conquers an enemy already defeated.*

Your Strengths + Good Work = Not Enough

It's the same for both men and women. Good work isn't enough. The difference is that, generally speaking, men know this and women don't.

Nancy Fredericks noticed a pattern in her business coaching. Concepts like looking for ways to manage up to impress superiors and networking outside of the company were easy for men. These came naturally to them. But the women she coached held to the belief that doing good work—great work even—is enough to climb the corporate ladder, thank you very much.

The men have it right. It's essential to build relationships with senior people and cultivate a comfort level if you want to move up in your organization. Success is not only about the caliber of your work.

Most companies deem establishing broad and deep professional relationships and playing by the interpersonal rules important. By contrast, female-oriented traits aren't usually on the list of factors considered most heavily in career advancement. Skills like intuition, nurturing others, and interpreting verbal and nonverbal communications may well have been very important throughout your career trajectory, but they won't help you be sufficiently recognized for your work. To play the game, you have to work the network.

Change Your Perceptions of Networking

Not surprisingly—given this disparity in the perceived importance of networking—authors Candy Deemer and Nancy Fredericks note that the sexes approach it quite differently. Men tend to see networking as part and parcel of playing the game, but women are prone to seeing it as based on false motives. "Women . . . often view networking as an illegitimate way to move around the businesses game board—a disingenuous form of relationship building, based on selfish motives and false feelings. Almost unanimously the women we have coached say they would rather be promoted based on their work than their connections," conclude the authors.

Developing and deepening relationships through out-of-company networking and managing up puts you in a favorable position. All things being equal, the promotion will come to the person with the better relationships, the person the boss shared a golf cart with, the person with the personal connection. All things being less equal, the promotion will still go to the person with the relationship. You're exponentially more likely to be hired away to a better position by a competitor you shared lunch with at a conference than one who didn't know you were on the market.

This is all about being positioned advantageously, something Sun Tzu believes in deeply: *Generally, he who occupies the field of battle first and awaits his enemy is at ease; he who arrives later and joins battle in haste is weary. And, therefore, one skilled in war brings the enemy to the field of battle and is not brought there by him.*

No-Power Networking

For many women, connections are the make-or-break factor in their success, says Sharon Hadary, founding executive director of the Center for Women's Business Research. Drawing conclusions based on what she's seen in focus groups, seminars, and in her experiences, Hadary believes the majority of women are not well-enough connected to use and receive credible introductions into networks like industry associations, chambers of commerce, and venture capital groups. She puts it plainly: "When women venture into diverse networks, they too often are not taken seriously and frequently are shut out of conversations and deals."

Because of this, women relegate themselves to organizations that don't benefit them in any real business sense. For example, Hadary says networking based on community groups and women's entrepreneurship networks is limiting.

She offers some advice. "The most successful women business owners join multiple, diverse networks to learn from their industry contacts, meet customers and develop connections to expertise. Having a critical mass of women in these networks helps women gain credibility, so women should reach out to other women and bring them into the networks," Hadary believes.

Shameless Self-Promotion

In addition to leveraging networks better, men also tend to be superior to women in promoting their successes, taking credit, and accepting praise. This is ironic, considering the preponderance of women who work in communications, marketing, and promotional fields. Many women are excellent publicity hounds for their organizations, their executives, or their clients, but when it comes to turning the lens on themselves, drawing attention to their victories and taking credit, they fail to reap the benefits.

If you fall into this category, and you won't promote yourself and your accomplishments, who will? You can't expect others to always notice. You need to artfully ensure that they do.

Great work is rarely enough. As Sun Tzu says, again, move first to get the superior position. Apply this ideology to influence your professional relationships and be prepared to seize opportunities: *Generally, in battle and maneuvering, all armies prefer high ground to low, and sunny places to shady. If an army encamps close to water and grass with adequate supplies, it will be free from countless diseases and this will spell victory. When you come to hills, dikes, or embankments, occupy the sunny side, with your main flank at the back. All these methods are advantageous to the army and can exploit the possibilities the ground offers.*

When you're well positioned, you will *miss no opportunity to defeat the enemy* and advance your cause.

When the Time Is Right, Trust Yourself

Follow the wisdom of *The Art of War*, adjust your strategies and tactics accordingly, and you'll be ready for any battle. When that time is at hand, all there is to do is to act. You'll bring forth your genuine self. You won't need to attempt to appear as something you're not, unless that's part of your strategy. Your essence will be revealed and your actions will take shape with the timing, speed, precision, and force required. As explained in Chapter 10: "Authenticity," you'll be one with your actions.

Sun Tzu repeatedly counsels that victory doesn't occur based on numbers alone. This applies to the larger, stronger, better-equipped, and better-entrenched opponents you face. Preparation, knowledge of the enemy, solid strategy and execution, and strength of spirit can overtake your opponent thoroughly, if you move when the time is right.

Your character is intrinsic. The battlefield is wherever you are. With years of experience, earnest desire, excellence in practice, and self-belief, you can hone your energy to create a leadership presence that's palpable to others.

BATTLEFIELD CHALLENGE

1. Think of a battle you fought, but that you shouldn't have. What did you learn from that experience? How can you personalize Sun Tzu's criteria to determine which battles to fight, which to postpone, and which to avoid entirely?

2. Identify some "little things" that are critical in your work but that you've been taking for granted. Does the renewed emphasis from the section "Everything Is Critical" challenge you to raise your standards?

3. How good are you at accepting praise or taking credit for accomplishments? Do you tend to quickly downplay it? What impact would it make if you stepped up and took credit more liberally?

WOMAN WARRIOR

Elizabeth I: "Oh Lord! The Queen Is a Woman!"

Elizabeth I possessed great battlefield wisdom. She embodied many of the qualities heralded by Sun Tzu. Chiefly, she got results. She defeated the unvanquished Spanish Armada in 1588 and reigned during an English golden age.

But her success was not a foregone conclusion. She overcame tremendous obstacles to become and remain queen, not the least of which was her decision to reign alone. As one citizen put it upon seeing Elizabeth after her coronation, "Oh Lord! The queen is a woman!"

The queen didn't engage in war unless she believed it was necessary. But when she did fight, she fought smart. She defied parliament and used hit-and-run tactics on the vulnerable Spanish rather than all-out war. She carefully chose political battles and steered clear of religious differences between Catholics and Protestants. Although deeply religious, she knew England needed consensus.

Elizabeth was prepared for the challenges she'd face. Smart and very well educated, she was also expert at judging character. This was part of the survival instincts she honed during a very difficult upbringing, which included the execution of her mother. She overcame fear and resisted intimidation throughout her life. More than a survivor, she was a victor.

Elizabeth always projected strength. Despite frequent illnesses, she avoided public signs of weakness. She knew how to make a mighty impression within the culture of the day. Elizabeth purposefully embodied the courtly tradition of the feminine ideal with pale skin, fair hair, and a graceful demeanor.

She was astutely aware of the people she led. In the midst of the Protestant Reformation, she knew that Roman Catholics highly regarded, even worshiped, the Virgin Mary. Converted Protestants had a void left by the diminished place of Mary, which had been such an essential part of their lives. Elizabeth craftily set about to fill this with her image of the "Virgin Queen." She blended royal and religious ideals and built broad support.

Elizabeth demonstrated concern for her people. When her court traveled, it was an uncomfortable and expensive undertaking that required 400 wagons. But every summer she traveled the land. She went to her soldiers, too. The night before an anticipated invasion by the Spanish, Elizabeth addressed her troops while donning the body armor of a cavalry officer. This was risky and exposed her to assassination. But she believed the greater danger was to be distant from the men. She told them, and showed them, she'd die with them. They believed her.

Chapter 17

Continuous Learning

孫子

Learning is not attained by chance, it must be sought for with ardor and attended to with diligence.
—ABIGAIL ADAMS

> **THE BATTLE:** Pride, complacency, and burnout can put you in a dangerous position—stuck right where you are. If you don't make ongoing learning an important part of your evolution, you'll never realize what you're capable of achieving.
>
> **THE CHAMPION:** Look to learn and grow at every opportunity. Continuously improve basic and advanced concepts and enhance your battlefield wisdom. If you understand the value of ongoing learning, your accomplishments will be unlimited.

Sun Tzu, like a serious athlete, never stops training. If you're an athlete who stops training, even briefly, you lose timing. Your speed and coordination rapidly deteriorate. In a matter of weeks, not months, your ability to respond well is diminished. You're no longer able to move with as much ease. You become less agile and flexible. Movements you've repeatedly practiced so they become second nature are now, once again, laborious. But most of all, it's your confidence that's shaken. You lose faith in what you can do. From here, defeat lies ahead.

Sun Tzu's general consistently pursues two mutually beneficial states at all times. The first state is beyond excellence. It's an ideal of enlightenment, foresight, and perfection.

The second state is the less ethereal, more terrestrial condition of studying himself, the enemy, his men, the field of battle, and all past, present, and future conditions. For Sun Tzu, a requirement of leadership is this active state of always seeking and executing ideal attacks and responses. Such discipline demands many attributes, not the least of which is openness to learning.

The Art of War advocates always seeking to learn and improve. When Sun Tzu guides you to leverage extraordinary and normal forces in battle to create an infinite variety of maneuvers, he's talking about the same type of continuity you must apply to ongoing personal growth: *It is like moving in a circle, never coming to an end. Who can exhaust the possibilities of their combinations?*

Empty Your Cup

Of course, not everyone believes they have much to learn. People at all levels can one day stop learning because they think they've seen it all and done it all. Others never allow themselves to grow and learn much at all. Whether it's fear, complacency, laziness, or arrogance that stands in our way, we can all learn something from the following parable.

Long ago, a young student in rural China travels to the home of a revered old kung fu master. He seeks to be accepted as the master's student. The young man longs to collect knowledge, to be a great fighter, to be admired and revered by many.

When the student arrives, the old master agrees to an impromptu private session.

They begin the lesson. The young man is eager to impress the master with his knowledge. Before the master teaches much, the young man tells him of the difficult moves he's studied, the instructors he's trained with, and the feats he's accomplished. The old master says little, but as all old masters do, listens.

After the practice, the old master invites the young man to join him for tea. Anticipating that his performance and knowledge have paid off and that the master will accept him as a student, the young man eagerly accepts. The master prepares the tea and slowly pours from the pot into the young man's cup. He pours until the cup is full, then keeps pouring as it overflows onto the floor. He continues to pour.

Startled, the young man says, "Master, master, stop. Look! You're spilling tea all over the floor!"

The master stops pouring and looks sternly at the youth. "If you are to learn something new, you must first empty your cup," he says.

A Paradigm for Learning

You probably meet people all the time who are sure they know everything. They've stopped learning. They believe they've accumulated enough knowledge. They no longer need to listen, either. If you treat each day as a new opportunity to grow better at what you do, these people with full cups are great to have as competitors. While they're standing still, you're studying and bettering yourself.

In many years of teaching martial arts, I've grown to be able to quickly identify the people who will stick around versus those who will attend a class or two and never be heard from again. The ones who, once shown a technique, say, "Oh, okay, but at the school I used to go to, we did it like this," will not be long-term students. They want only to be immersed in a paradigm that fits their comfort level. They're fearful of learning something new, because that causes them to call into question the absolute validity of their experiences and knowledge.

Whether it's the Chinese countryside or an office on Wall Street, the people who know it all are the ones who will learn the least. Their cup is already full. They are unwilling to empty it for a time to learn something new.

Sharpen the Blade

"Sharpening the saw" is Stephen Covey's excellent way of saying that you have to take time for renewal, which he describes in *The 7 Habits of Highly Effective People*. Covey's analogy involves someone who's been working for five hours to saw down a tree. Rather than stopping briefly to sharpen the saw and make his labor more effective, he continues on in his slow, laborious quest. He has a goal and he's fixed upon it. He doesn't have the time, he says, to stop, not even to sharpen the saw. It's too bad, because sharpening the saw would make his efforts so much more effective.

Since we're delving into time-tested battlefield wisdom, we'll adapt Covey's analogy to use the blade of a sword instead of a saw. Blunted weapons lead to destruction for Sun Tzu: *If the war is long delayed, the men's weapons will be blunted and their ardor will be dampened. . . . Now, when your weapons are blunted, your ardor dampened, your strength exhausted and your treasure spent, neighboring rulers will take advantage of your distress to act. In this case, no man, however wise, is able to avert the disastrous consequences that ensue.*

Achieving excellence demands a razor-sharp blade. It requires training and learning, and always being in a state of renewal, improvement, and refinement.

When it comes to launching an attack and being prepared to defend yourself, the condition of the blade is especially important. If it's dull, you'll be working a lot harder and getting less and less in return. The more effort you expend, the less return you'll receive. Despite the potential it has when well-maintained, a dull sword won't do what it's supposed to do. This will become obvious to others. Enemies will overtake you. Colleagues will have to carry you. Superiors will learn not to rely on you.

The more effort you put into keeping the blade sharp and maintaining the sword when you're not in the midst of battle, the less effort you'll have to put forth when it's showtime.

Sometimes you have no choice but to stop and sharpen the blade. When eBay experienced a major site outage in 1999, Meg Whitman had to quickly come up to speed on the technologies behind the auction house. She had only begun to learn that part of the business, but moved into the site operations center with a team of engineers for almost the entire summer.

Round It Out

As Sun Tzu advises, you must be able to fight in many scenarios. To do this, you must always freshly evaluate your offensive and defensive strategy and execution: *Those who are skilled in defense hide themselves as under the most secret recesses of earth. Those skilled in attack flash forth as from above the topmost heights of heaven. Thus, they are capable both of protecting themselves and of gaining a complete victory.*

This evaluation requires you to consider your areas of weakness as well as your strengths. Learning about and improving your areas of vulnerability are essential to achieving success.

Consider Nadia, a small business owner who churned through salespeople. In those frequent periods between salespeople, she had to do the selling herself. The problem was that she hated to sell. So her team would execute marketing programs that would drive leads, but she couldn't do the follow-up necessary to make the programs effective. The wasted costs, dropped leads, and overall damage to her business were irreparable. It's not important that everyone can do everything in your organization, but it's important that at least the essential bases are covered.

What Is Learned Is More Important than What Is Taught

To actively pursue learning, you must know what you know, know what you don't know, and set goals for how you'll develop the knowledge you need to reach the next level. You must take ownership of learning. Carly Fiorina put it like this: "Every experience in life, whether humble or grand, teaches a lesson. The question is not if the lesson is taught, but rather if it is learned."

I've been fortunate enough to have some great teachers in many pursuits in my life. My jujitsu instructor, Randy Hutchins, has been the best. Not only is he an incredibly gifted, off-the-charts practitioner, he's also a skilled and compassionate teacher. The two don't always go together. That's what makes him so special.

When it comes to learning the complex underpinnings of jujitsu, I've always been about as thick as Sensei Hutchins is gifted. He would explain movements, concepts, and directions to me. After practicing repetitively, I'd be lucky if some portion of them got through.

Early in my training, Sensei had a couple of students who would teach for him on rare occasions when he wasn't there. One such night, one of his seniors, George, worked with me on a locking throw called *kote gaeshi*. If the lock is done correctly, it hurts and the attacker has no choice but to go where you put him, which, if he's lucky, is flat onto his back. I was several months into jujitsu training, so I really only knew enough to get myself hurt. I was having a hard time with *kote gaeshi*, especially since you have to make large, sweeping movements with your legs while coordinating your upper body and blending with the attacker to move him. It's even more complicated than it sounds.

It was just George and me that night, so I had his undivided attention. We practiced *kote gaeshi* over and over again. While George had only had a couple of years of jujitsu experience, he helped me understand the technique better than ever before. His explanation enabled me to understand it in a whole new way. For the first time, the concepts of the technique came together, and I began to perform it more smoothly and effortlessly.

I couldn't wait to share with Sensei how well I'd learned, and my new revelation. I also wondered why Sensei hadn't explained these concepts to me. After all, he taught them to George, who taught them to me. When I saw Sensei a few days later I explained George's masterful explanation. I thought he would be impressed that I finally understood.

His reply wasn't what I had expected. "I know," he nodded nonchalantly. "I've been telling you the same thing for months. Sometimes it just takes another person or another approach for it to sink in."

Sensei had taught me the same thing that George had, but I hadn't learned it until I received George's explanation, approach, and undivided attention. But even more important was the timing. It had finally been right for this understanding to take root. And since then, countless other levels of understanding regarding that single technique have emerged for me—when the time was right.

The Time for Learning

It's not just me. My students sometimes don't get a concept for months or even years. They may perform the movement, but they miss the essence of the technique. Then, on day fifty-seven of practicing it, the student will finally get the concept I've been trying to explain for some time. Their time to learn had not been right until then.

You can't force understanding on others and expect it to take root. It grows in its own time and on its own schedule. This holds true for every lesson you'll learn in life. Whether it's a new position or new responsibilities, you can't pick it all up right away. The more valuable lessons are often learned over time. Cultivation of skill requires patience and perseverance.

Be a Patient Teacher

Some bosses see themselves as professors, teaching their employees how to be as smart as they are. This is commendable, assuming that the boss has worthwhile knowledge to share. But the act of teaching is far less important than the knowledge the employee can apply.

This is true in all of communications. What you say and how you say it is far less important than being able to read the person on the other side of the table and make your message resonate. Use your feminine skills in picking up on verbal and nonverbal cues when you're teaching and training others.

Willingness to Learn from "Inferiors"

Personal growth requires humility, and pride prevents personal growth. It's appropriate to learn from superiors and bosses. We're supposed to get smarter as a result of what they tell us and show us. After all, they're in superior positions for a reason. Of course, at some point in our careers, most of us have had managers and supervisors who we didn't think had that much to teach. Maybe you share the sentiments of *Naked in the Boardroom* author Robin Wolaner when she says, "My best mentors have been antimentors, the men whose behavior taught me what not to do."

That notwithstanding, learning from managers and leaders is natural. But it's more difficult to learn from "inferiors," the ones underneath us. Even so, it's worthwhile to be attentive for opportunities.

When I met my husband, I had been training in martial arts for nearly ten years. He had never so much as gone to a single lesson. When he decided he wanted to do jujitsu, I was thrilled. I'd have a training partner, which was especially valuable since, at that time, I had to travel over one hundred and fifty miles one way to attend class.

But Dave wasn't just any training partner. I'm five feet five inches tall. He's six feet two inches. He easily outweighed me by a hundred pounds. To top it all off, he was very stiff. With a joint locking martial art, this posed a number of challenges. He thought I was trying to hurt him. I thought he was stubbornly trying to resist techniques.

As time went by, we worked together more frequently. I was at a point of new growth in my training. I had black belts in several different martial arts, and I had high expectations of myself. Because jujitsu is very practical, it's very clear when a technique isn't working. When I'd go to throw or lock Dave, if I didn't do it properly, he wouldn't move. I would then become frustrated with myself and angry at him. As Sun Tzu tells us, anger and frustration are hindrances.

At these times, I was not open to listening and learning. My head was too full of anger, resentment, and disappointment. That's makes for one very full, very useless cup. While Dave had far less experience than I did, he's a smart guy and he has an excellent intuition about body mechanics and jujitsu. But I wouldn't listen to his observations. How could he possibly know as much as I did?

Who was the stubborn one now?

Listen (Even) When You Don't Want To

Gradually I learned to listen to Dave, and my skill improved as a result. Rather than becoming defensive when he would suggest a means of modifying a technique to deal with his body type, I listened. It turns out that he was often on the right track.

Learning to listen wasn't an overnight process. It took some time and a very healthy dose of humility. I had to be open to receiving information without preconceived ideas. I learned to take myself out of the way so I didn't miss a valuable source of knowledge.

Ideas come from even the most unlikely sources. If you allow your prejudices to color your perceptions, you may discount some very good contributions along the way. There are better, stronger, smarter, and more capable people out there. You can choose to ignore what they bring to the table, or you can leverage it.

The best teachers are the ones who will tell you they're still learning. The truly great will even share with you that they learn from the people they teach. This includes beginners. For these experts, learning is a conscious and active process. They're always looking to learn, even in teaching. They know enough to know they don't know everything.

BATTLEFIELD CHALLENGE

1. If you're having a problem staying motivated, ask yourself when it was that you were last fired up. What inspired you, and how can you re-create those conditions? It may take drastic measures, but the benefits will outweigh the short-term discomfort.

2. To put continuous learning into practice, go back to the weaknesses you identified in the Battlefield Challenge at the end of Chapter 13. What areas are in most need of focused learning? What steps will you take to round out your skills?

3. Think about a time when you modeled the young man in the section titled "Empty Your Cup." When have you had to temporarily sideline your knowledge to make room for a new lesson? What was the result?

Meg Whitman Practices Learning at Every Opportunity

Meg Whitman's distinguished career has been defined by learning along the way and brilliantly putting these lessons into practice. When she stepped into leadership at eBay, the online auction house had twenty employees. Ten years later, she left a publicly traded global powerhouse boasting $8 billion in revenue.

For Whitman, excellence in learning and leading comes from knowing you can't know everything. She's been called a consensus CEO. She listens to vested interests and makes decisions accordingly. "What will kill a growth company is someone who can't make decisions. But you have to listen very hard, recognize which constituencies are speaking and then make a decision for the greater good," she says.

Whitman candidly acknowledges mistakes. In the early days eBay may have made decisions too quickly, and made miscalculations in pricing, user interface, and strategy. But the company ultimately triumphed over these problems with smart and rapid solutions based on lessons learned and input from critical parties.

One hurdle was eBay Motors. The initiative was successful at first, but eBay then made user interface changes independently of the community's knowledge. These changes compromised its success and disrupted users. As a measure of the uproar, Whitman received about 5,000 e-mails the day changes were made.

Of the famous eBay site outage in June of 1999, she said it was a learning experience and growth opportunity. She led by being on-site during this critical time, essentially moving into the site operations center. The facility was stocked with cots, sleeping bags, pillows, toothbrushes, toothpaste, and other personal items for the people who worked through the summer. "It was a crash course in technology which has served me in good stead since," she reflects.

Whitman also learned from users and partners. She directed eBay to go to its channel partners and ask how the auction website could enhance their businesses. In the tradition of Sun Tzu, her success comes from a constant study of the conditions of battle and thorough understanding of allies.

Going Forward •

The experiences of Whitman, Fiorina, Rice, Covey, Nooyi, and many others show us the relevance of Sun Tzu for today's female leaders. No matter where you are in your professional journey, you can readily adapt his battlefield principles for tremendous results. The question is: How will you apply the timeless wisdom of *The Art of War* to shape your future?

Bibliography

Abrams, Susan L. *The New Success Rules for Women*. (Roseville, CA: Prima Publishing, 2000).

PBS Online. Africans in America: People & Events: Harriet Tubman. *www.pbs.org/wgbh/aia/part4/4p1535.html*.

Ashby, Ruth and Deborah Gore Ohrn, Editors. *Herstory, Women Who Changed the World*. (New York, NY: Viking, 1995).

Associated Press. "Harvard Board Names First Woman President," February 11, 2007.

Axelrod, Alan. *Elizabeth I CEO: Strategic Lessons from the Leader Who Built an Empire*. (Paramus, NJ: Prentice Hall Press, 2000).

Azar, Beth. "A New Stress Paradigm for Women," *Monitor on Psychology*, July 2000.

Babcock, Linda and Sara Laschever. *Women Don't Ask: Negotiation and the Gender Divide*. (Princeton and Oxford: Princeton University Press, 2003).

Brem, Marion Luna. *Women Make the Best Salesmen*. (New York, London, Toronto, Sydney, Auckland: Double Day Publishers, 2005).

Brady, Diane. "Indra Nooyi: Keeping Cool In Hot Water," *Businessweek*, June 11, 2007.

Brown, Mary Beth. *Condi: The Life of a Steel Magnolia*. (Nashville, Dallas, Mexico City, Rio De Janeiro: Thomas Nelson, 2007).

Burke, Steven and Heather Clancy. "Meg Whitman," *CRN*, November 15, 2004.

Center for Women's Business Research. "The Economic Impact of Women-Owned Businesses In the United States," October 2009.

Center for Women's Business Research. "Decision Making Styles of Women Business Owners Differs from Male Business Owners," June 13, 2006.

Coolidge, Shelley Donald. "Trading 30,000 Staff For 3 Kids," *The Christian Science Monitor*, October 8, 1997.

Condren, Debra, PhD. *Ambition Is Not a Dirty Word: A Woman's Guide to Earning Her Worth and Achieving Her Dreams*. (New York, NY: Morgan Road Books, 2006).

Coontz, Stephanie. "Myth of the Opt-Out Mom," *The Christian Science Monitor*, March 30, 2006.

Covey, Stephen R. *The 7 Habits of Highly Effective People*. (New York, NY: Simon & Schuster, Inc., 2004).

DeBaise, Colleen. "Special Report: Ladies First," *Smart Money*, November 30, 2006.

Deemer, Candy and Nancy Fredericks. *Dancing on the Glass Ceiling.* (New York, NY: McGraw Hill, 2002).

DiSesa, Nina. *Seducing the Boys Club.* (New York, NY: Ballantine Books, 2008).

Fiorina, Carly. *Tough Choices, A Memoir.* (New York, NY: Penguin Group, 2006).

Fiorina, Carly. "Making the Best of a Mess," *New York Times*, September 29, 1999.

Fiorina, Carly. "Fiorina's Commencement Address," *Businessweek*, May 7, 2005.

Frankel, Lois, P., PhD. *See Jane Lead—99 Ways for Women to Take Charge at Work.* (New York, Boston: Warner Business Books, 2007).

Goudreah, Jenna. "Building a Business on Scrap," *Forbes*, May 1, 2009.

Gumpel, Eve. "There's No Easy Path to Success," *Women Entrepreneur*, October 30, 2008.

Gurian, Michael with Barbara Annis. *Leadership and the Sexes: Using Gender Science to Create Success in Business.* (San Francisco, CA: Jossey-Bass, 2008).

Goudreau, Jenna. "Patricia Russo Is Saving America, One Board At A Time," *Forbes*, January 19, 2010.

Grove, Lloyd. "World According to Geraldine Laybourne," *Portfolio. com*, January 24, 2008.

Hadary, Sharon G. "Why Are Women-Owned Firms Smaller Than Men-Owned Ones?" *Wall Street Journal*, May 17, 2010.

Hazell, Rebecca. *Heroines: Great Women Through the Ages.* (New York, NY: Abbeville Publishing Group, 1996).

Heffernan, Margaret. *How She Does It: How Women Entrepreneurs Are Changing the Rules of Business Success.* (New York, NY: Viking, 2007).

Hyams, Joe. The Bruce Lee Foundation, "Knowing Is Not Enough," Fall 2000.

The Internet Movie Database (www.imdb.com/title/tt0070034/quotes), *Enter the Dragon*, starring Bruce Lee, in a conversation with an older member of the temple, 1973.

Harvard Law Bulletin, Summer 2002.

Jones, Del. "Women CEOs Slowly Gain on Corporate America," *USA Today*, January 2, 2009.

Kalinosky, Evelyn. "Feeling Like A Fraud: Living With Impostor Syndrome," *Forbes*, February 22, 2010.

Khaldoun, Ibn. *History of the Berbers and the Muslim Dynasties in Northern Africa.* (Berti, Algiers: 2003).

Koselka, Rita. "A Real Amazon," *Forbes*, April 5, 1999.

Krowl, Michelle A. *Women Who Dare: Women of the Civil War.* (Petaluma, CA: Pomegranate, 2006).

Krull, Kathleen. *Lives of Extraordinary Women: Rules, Rebels (and What the Neighbors Thought).* (San Diego, New York, London: Harcourt, Inc., 2001).

Lafayette de Mente, Boye. *Samurai Strategies: 42 Martial Secrets from Musashi's Book of Five Rings.* (North Clarendon, VT: Tuttle Publishing, 2005).

Lee, Bruce. *Tao of Jeet Kune Do.* (Valencia, CA: Ohara Publications, 1975).

Lowry, Dave. *Moving Toward Stillness: Lessons in Daily Life from the Martial Ways of Japan.* (Boston, MA: Tuttle Publishing, 2000).

Ludeman, Kate and Eddie Erlandson. *Alpha Male Syndrome.* (Boston: Harvard Business School Press, 2006).

Mendell, Adrienne. *How Men Think.* (New York, NY: Ballantine Books, 1996).

Michaelson, Gerald A. and Steven Michaelson. *Sun Tzu: The Art of War for Managers: 50 Strategic Rules Updated for Today's Businesses.* (Avon, MA: Adams Media, 2010).

Musashi, Miyamoto and Thomas Cleary. *The Book of Five Rings.* (Boston, MA: Shambhala Publications, Inc., 1993).

Nathan, Amy. *Count On Us: American Women in the Military.* (Washington, DC: National Geographic Society, 2004).

National Foundation for Women Business Owners. "Entrepreneur Vision in Action: Exploring Growth Among Women- and Men-Owned Firms," February 2001.

National Institute of Mental Health. "Gender Differences in Behavioral Responses to Stress: 'Fight or Flight' Vs 'Tend and Befriend,'" December 1, 2003.

Nelston, Sharon. "A Scrappy Entrepreneur," *U.S. Chamber of Commerce*, June 1997.

Rimer, Sara. "A 'Rebellious Daughter' to Lead Harvard," *New York Times*, February 12, 2007.

Roberts, David. *Once They Moved Like the Wind: Cochise, Geronimo, and the Apache Wars*. (New York, NY: Touchstone, 1994).

SCORE. "Stats on Women in Business," *www.score.org/women_stats .html*.

Shaw, Ian. *The Oxford History of Ancient Egypt*. (Oxford University Press, 2000).

Thomas, Cathy Booth. "A Woman's Burden," *Time*, March 28, 2003.

United States Small Business Administration. "FAQs," September 2009, *www.sba.gov/advo/stats/sbfaq.pdf*.

Useem, Michael. "America's Best Leaders: Indra Nooyi, PepsiCo CEO," *U.S. News & World Report*, November 19, 2008.

Vasquez, Tina. "Voice of Experience: Elaine Sarsynski, Executive Vice President, MassMutual's Retirement Services Division and Chairman and Chief Executive Officer, MassMutual International LLC," *The Glass Hammer*, April 19, 2010.

Vogelstein, Fred. "Carly Fiorina Tells Her Story," *Wired*, October 9, 2006.

Walker, Elaine. "Ex-Macy's Exec Sue Kronick Reflects on Corporate Life," *Miami Herald*, May 24, 2010.

Wallace, Amy, transcript of her interview in *Portfolio*. "Life After eBay: An Interview With Meg Whitman," *Seeking Alpha*, April 22, 2008.

Wiener, Tom. *Forever a Soldier: Unforgettable Stores of Wartime Service*. (Washington, DC: National Geographic Society, 2006).

Wolaner, Robin. *Naked in the Boardroom*. (New York, London, Toronto, Sydney: Simon & Schuster, 2005).

Women in History. "Wilma Rudolph Biography." Updated: March 9, 2010. Lakewood Public Library. Date accessed June 28, 2010. *www .lkwdpl.org/wihohio/rudo-wil.htm*.

Women's Business Research Center. "Key Facts about Women Owned Businesses," 2008–2009 Update. *www.womensbusinessresearchcenter .org/research/keyfacts*.

Index